A–Z

OF

POOLE

Places - People - History

Andrew Jackson

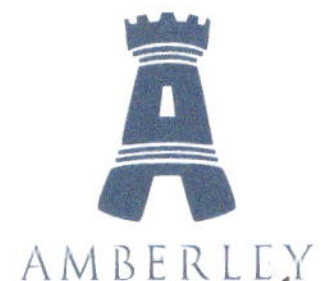

AMBERLEY

First published 2020

Amberley Publishing
The Hill, Stroud, Gloucestershire, GL5 4EP
www.amberley-books.com

Copyright © Andrew Jackson, 2020

The right of Andrew Jackson to be identified
as the Author of this work has been asserted in
accordance with the Copyrights, Designs and
Patents Act 1988.

ISBN 978 1 3981 0042 8 (print)
ISBN 978 1 3981 0043 5 (ebook)

British Library Cataloguing in Publication Data.
A catalogue record for this book is available
from the British Library.

Typesetting by SJmagic DESIGN SERVICES,
India. Printed in Great Britain.

Contents

Introduction

Poole is the veritable jewel in a bejewelled south coast crown. It is the world's second largest and Europe's largest natural harbour, with a hundred miles of coastline abounding with natural beauty. It is a wonderful haven for wildlife and birds, as well as an ideal spot for sailing and water sports enthusiasts.

Poole Bay consists of a 7-mile stretch of azure blue seas and golden sands, 3 miles of which lie within the Borough of Poole. On a sunny day, you feel you could be anywhere in the world, like the Caribbean or the Greek Islands. However, as with most British resorts, if you decide to plunge into the sea, that illusion is soon dispelled.

Nonetheless, the Poole and Bournemouth conurbation does seem to have a unique temperate microclimate which is frequently at odds with the rest of the British weather.

The most historic part of Poole is the Quay, which has been in use since Iron Age inhabitants survived on the harbour's plentiful supply of oysters, cockles, crabs and fish. It later became an important medieval port, and many of the medieval structures still remain.

The Quay today is a bustling working port, but also boasts many cafés and family attractions. However, the rich maritime heritage, involving Newfoundland traders, pirates and smugglers, is still apparent among the old seafront buildings and pubs, giving one the accurate impression that some of those walls could tell a few tales.

Just behind the Quay is a quarter known as the Old Town, which has a predominantly eighteenth-century feel, as this is where the merchants involved in the lucrative trade with Newfoundland built themselves some imposing mansions.

The A–Z format affords an opportunity to delve more deeply into these issues, and into the places and characters which are, as the town motto states, 'Ad Morem Villae de Poole' (according to the custom of the town of Poole).

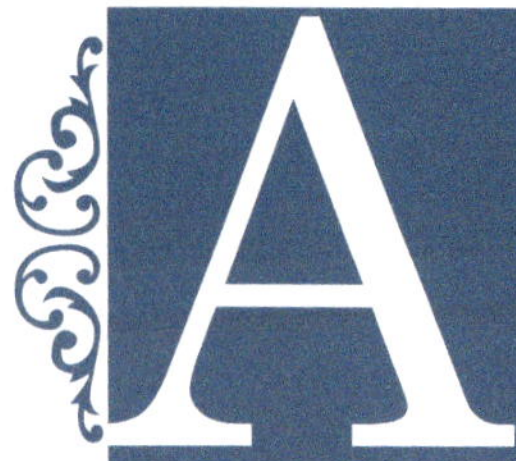

A

Almshouses

The Almshouses charity caters for past and present residents of Poole, or people who have connections to the Poole Pottery/Carters Tiles industries. Residents are accepted from sixty-five years of age.

The buildings date back to the early fifteenth century, and were built by the Fraternity of St George for the priests at St James' Church. They have been used as almshouses since 1586.

The brick gables and chimneys are seventeenth century, and there is a niche situated in the wall which housed Poole's first street lamp.

Almshouses.

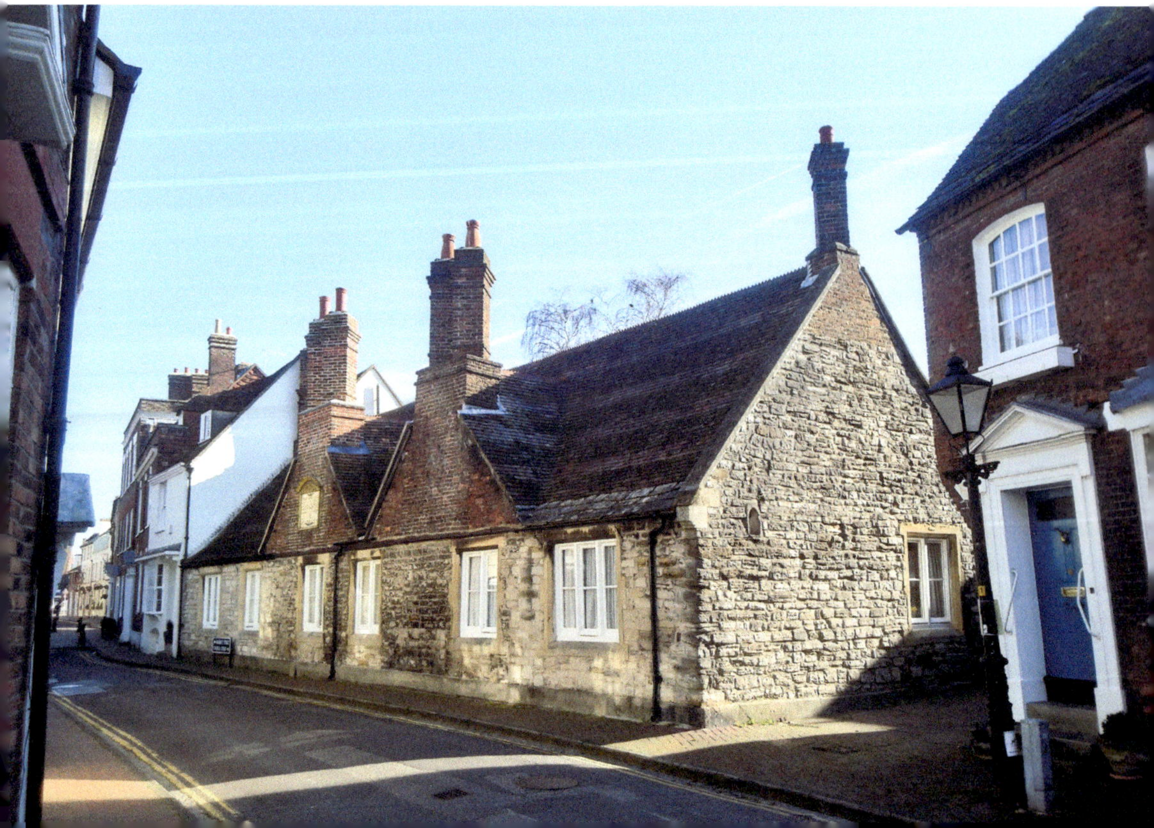

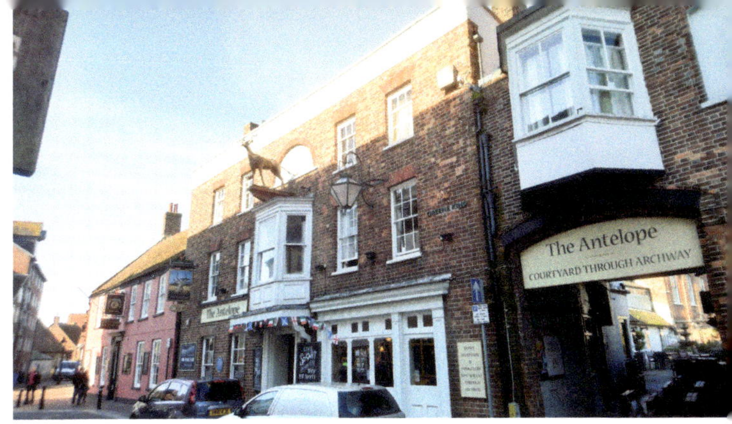

The Antelope.

Antelope

The Antelope dates back to 1465, and was originally named the Antelope Inn. It was a Royal Mail coaching inn, which in addition to the mail, took passengers to and from London, Bristol and Bath.

Some of the original artefacts of the building still remain, such as the massive Purbeck stone fireplace in the bar and the wooden beams.

To the rear of the hotel is a building that has seen many different uses over the years. At one time, it was a brewery providing beer for the pub. Other uses have included cargo storage for the Newfoundland trade, and an onion storage depot for the 'Johnny Onion' sellers from Roscoff in Brittany.

In the early nineteenth century, the building was refurbished with a Georgian frontage, and a second floor was added. During this period, the name was also changed to the Antelope Hotel, to distinguish it from another establishment which had opened in New Street called the New Antelope Inn. Later the prefix 'Old' was added, so it became the Old Antelope Hotel, thus distinguishing it further.

The upstairs rooms currently offer bed and breakfast accommodation, but in the past rooms have been used for meetings, as a ballroom, a sail loft and a judges' court.

At one time, the pub was used as a meeting point for the Poole lifeboat crew (see RNLI), and was also the headquarters for a unit of Second World War commandos known as the Small Scale Raiding Force. On one raid they were detailed to attack the Atlantic Wall, which was a series of fortifications built by the Nazis along the coast of Continental Europe. They were intercepted by German commandos en route, and in the ensuing skirmish, their leader, Captain Gus March-Phillips, was killed.

Artists

Poole has been the home of two of Britain's most influential artists: Augustus John and Henry Lamb.

Augustus John (1876–1961), was one of the towering figures of British art, and for a time around 1910, was one of the most important exponents of post-impressionism in Britain. He was also celebrated for his brilliant figure drawings.

He was born in Tenby, in Pembrokeshire, Wales, but lived and worked in Poole. He was well known for his bohemian lifestyle, and was a regular at the Nelson public house, where he enjoyed the company of the Romany gypsies who also frequented the Nelson at that time.

One of his most famous portraits was that of Lawrence of Arabia, which he painted in 1919. Lawrence was a friend, who also frequented both the Nelson and the Jolly Sailor, although he lived outside Poole at nearby Bovington, travelling on his motorbike.

Henry Lamb (1883–1960) was another famous artist who made Poole his home. He was born in Adelaide, Australia, but moved to Manchester as a young boy and later trained as a doctor, before studying at Chelsea Art College.

During the First World War, he served as a medic, and won the Military Cross for tending to injured soldiers whilst under heavy fire.

After the First World War, he followed his mentor at Chelsea Art College, Augustus John, to Poole where he painted many local scenes and landmarks. Perhaps his most famous painting was the *Level Crossing* painted in 1953, which is the level crossing in Poole High Street, still in operation today.

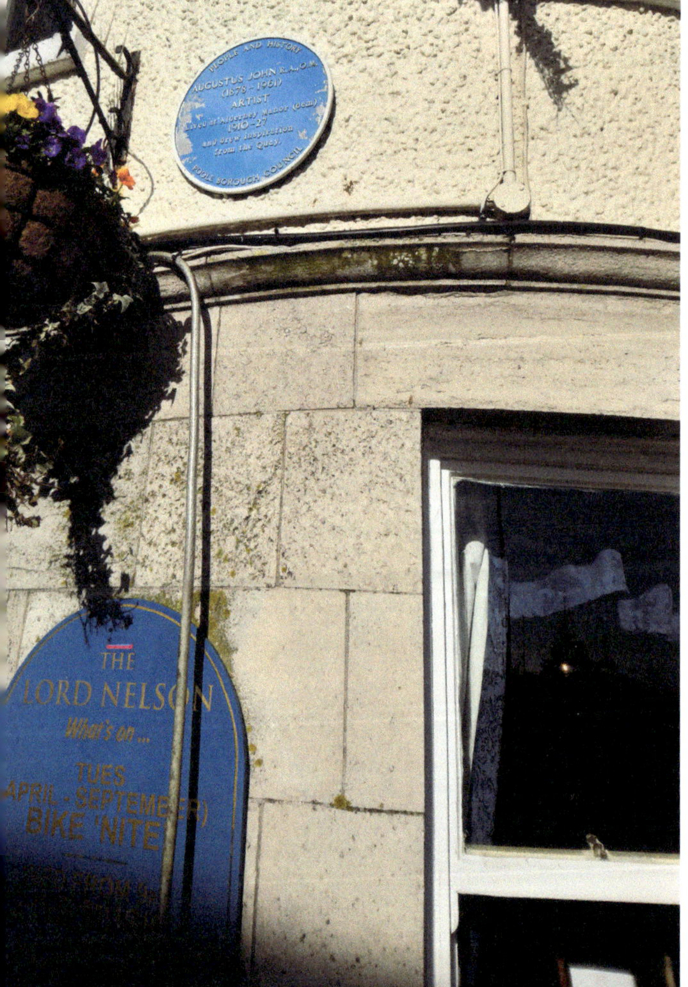

A plaque on the wall of the Lord Nelson pub in recognition of former regular patron Augustus John (artist).

Baden-Powell

Baden-Powell (1857–1941) learnt his scouting/tracking skills, whilst serving in the army, by observing tribesmen from around the world.

In 1899, he was posted to the Boer War in South Africa and was based in the town of Mafeking, which was under siege from the Boers. The British were outnumbered nine to one, and he had to use all his skills and resourcefulness to ensure that the town held out until it was relieved. One of the measures he took was to issue small boys with bicycles, so they could act as messengers. He came to value their efficiency and cheerfulness.

In 1904, Baden-Powell attended the twenty-first celebrations of the Boys Brigade and was asked to devise a scheme for giving greater variety in their training. The programme he devised was called Scouting for Boys, which the Boys Brigade only partially adopted. However, realising he was on to something, he contacted a friend who owned Brownsea Island, Charles van Raalte, and initiated the first scout camp.

Below left: A sculpture of Lord Baden-Powell by David A. Annan. The plaque reads: 'Robert Baden Powell OM 1st Baron of Gilwell and Freeman of the Borough of Poole. Founder of the Scout Movement. Poole – Where it all began.'

Below right: Scout Stone, Brownsea Island.

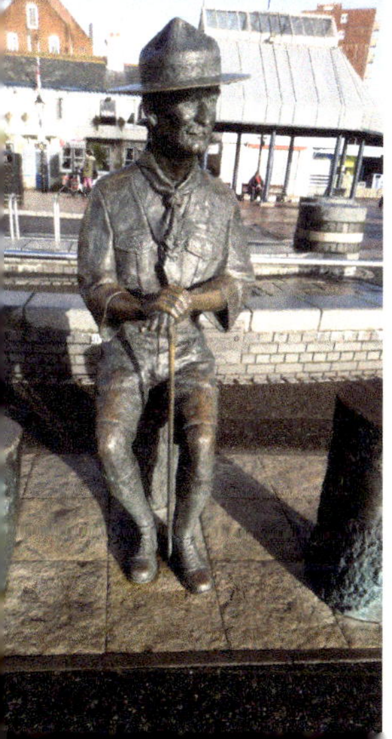

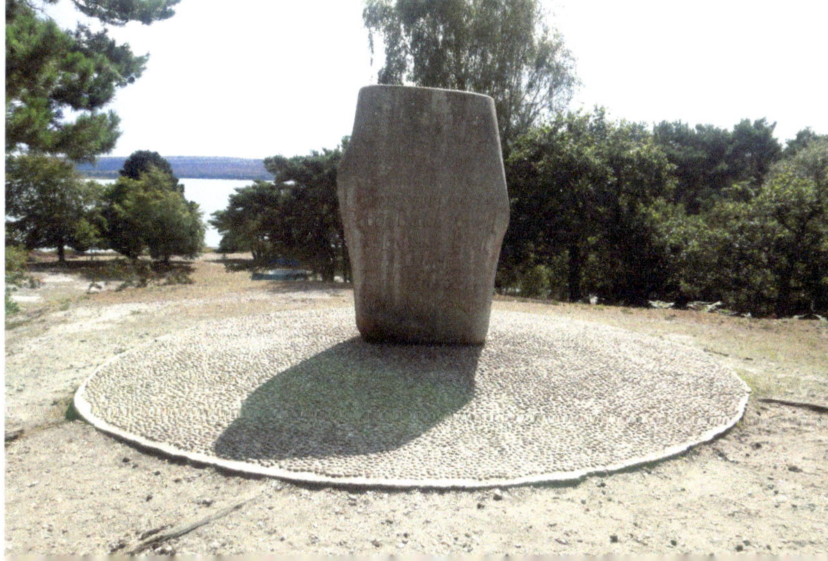

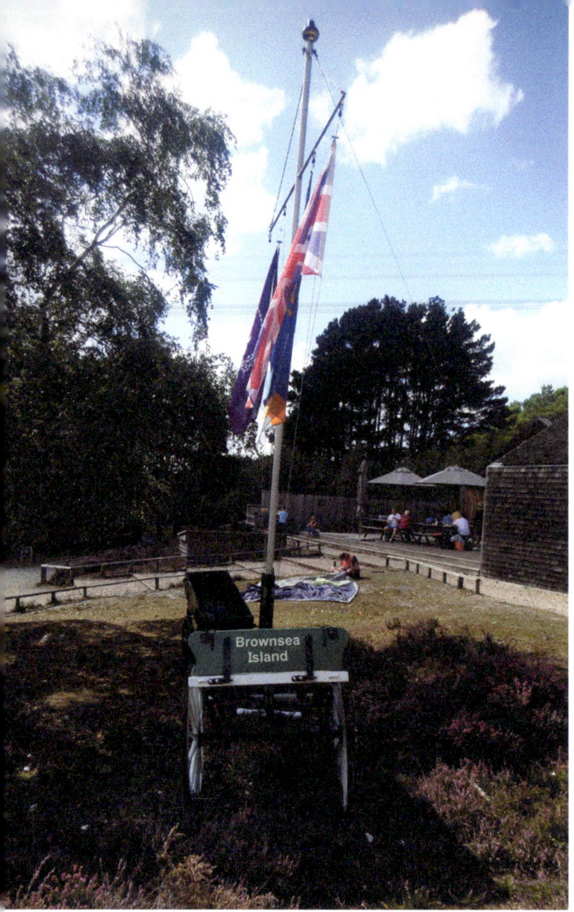

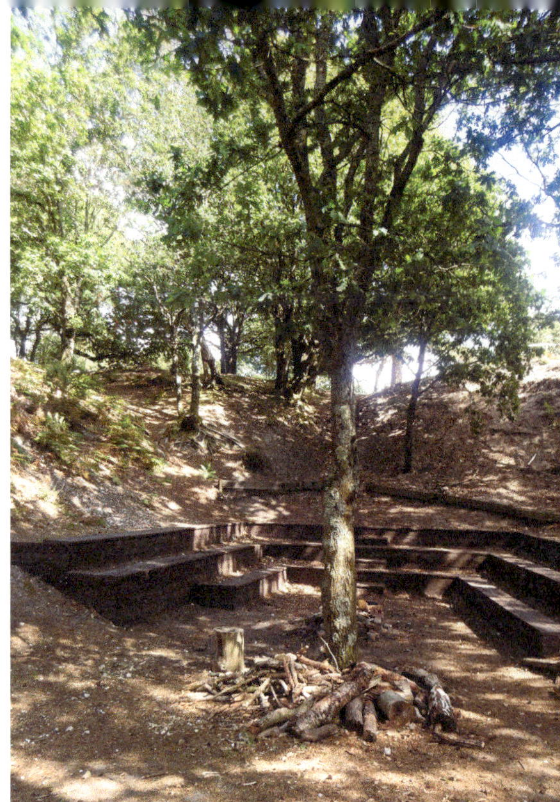

Above: Scout campfire circle, Brownsea Island.

Left: Scout campsite, Brownsea Island.

Baden-Powell wanted to discover what kind of boy would be interested in his scheme, so he invited pupils from public schools and those from working-class families, and also included both city and country dwellers.

Twenty-one boys, including three from Poole and seven from Bournemouth, were at Brownsea on 31 July 1907. They were divided into four patrols and spent their days learning and practising the skills of scouting, campcraft, cooking, observation, woodcraft, life-saving, hiking, stalking, and boating, etc., before retiring for campfires in the evening. The camp was a great success and was the catalyst for the scouting movement, which then, as today, had appeal for those of all backgrounds.

A stone on the island at the site of the first campsite commemorates the event, and 50 acres are set aside for use by the scouts for camping and scout-related activities. Today, there are 16 million scouts in 150 countries.

The Girl Guides were formed in 1910, by Baden-Powell's sister, Agnes Baden-Powell, and she also took the Guides to Brownsea for their first camp.

The centenary of scouting was celebrated on Brownsea in 2007, as scouts from all over the world came together for a jamboree. The Baden-Powell Outdoor Centre and Museum was also opened at this event.

Poole has another association with Baden-Powell as his wife, Olave Soames, was from Lilliput. They were married in St Peter's Church, Parkstone on 31 October 1912.

Baden-Powell was made a Freeman of Poole in 1929.

Beaches

Poole Bay, which stretches from Sandbanks to Southbourne, consists of 7 miles of natural golden sands and clear, clean water. The beaches within Poole Borough's 3-mile section are Sandbanks, Shore Road, Canford Cliffs, Branksome Chine and Branksome Dene Chine.

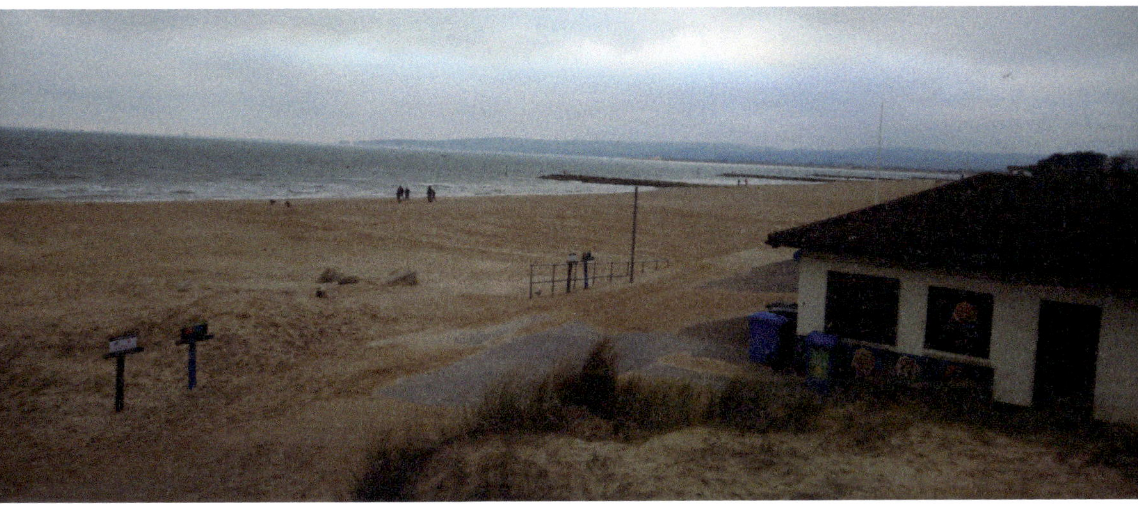

Above: Sandbanks Beach.

Right: Shore Road Beach.

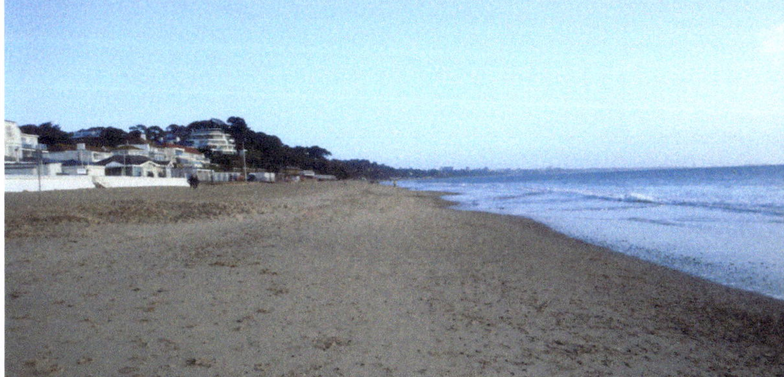

Canford Cliffs Beach.

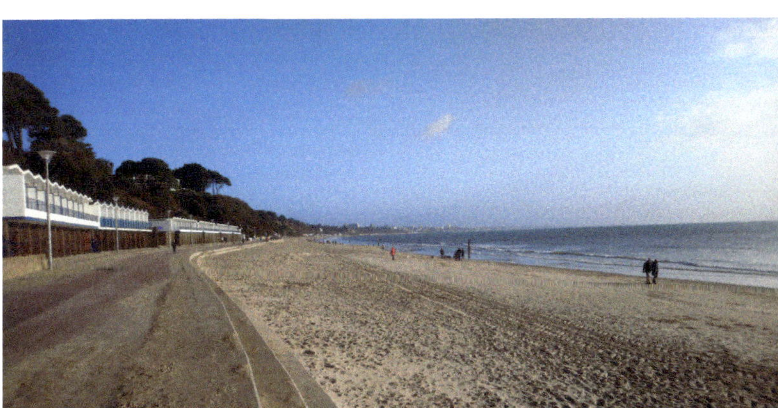

This stretch of coastline has won numerous blue flags, and Sandbanks has won more than any other British beach.

Other beaches situated within Poole Harbour, and within the Borough of Poole, include Harbour Lake, Rockley Sands and Sandbanks Harbour.

Birds

Holes Bay is a tidal inland lake which lies in the northern part of Poole Harbour.

In 2015, part of Holes Bay was designated as a European Marine Site (EMS), and a Special Protection Area (SPA), Site of Special Scientific Interest (SSSI). It is also a RAMSAR site (Ramsar is the name of the town in Iran where the international treaty for the preservation of wetland sites of international importance for the preservation of birds was signed), and plays host to many nationally and internationally important species of wetland birds and wildlife.

The extensive areas of shallow waters and marshland make Poole Harbour an important bird migration route, as it has an abundance of suitable food in the form of insects, mollusks, larvae, fish, crustaceans and ragworm. Birds and wildlife can be found on mudflats throughout the harbour, but the sheltered and enclosed nature of Holes Bay makes it a particularly safe and secluded environment.

Birds that may be seen frequently are oystercatchers, redshank, wigeon and dunlin, as well as many more unusual species. In the spring and autumn, the mudflats dotted around the harbour can be full of birds stopping to rest and recuperate before migrating to warmer climates.

From May to July, common sandwich terns, grey herons, little egrets, shelducks and kingfishers may be seen; whereas, in the winter migrating birds stop here to feed, including avocets and spoonbills.

In 2013, marsh harriers began breeding in the harbour again after a fifty-year absence. Redshanks, which have an amber status of European Species of Concern, also frequent the area.

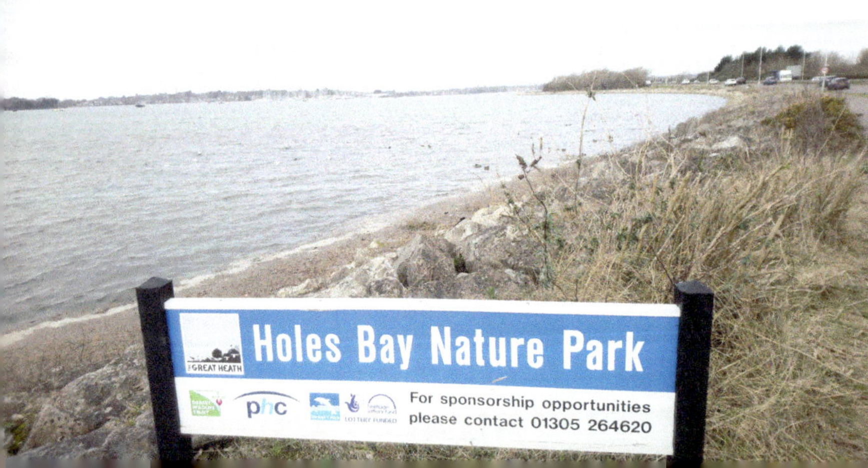

Holes Bay
Nature Park.

C

Cargo

Poole has been an industrial port for many years, and until the mid-eighteenth century, locally produced livestock, grain, vegetables, dairy produce, leather, wool and Purbeck stone were shipped to London and elsewhere. Poole Harbour clay was also supplied to the Staffordshire Potteries.

However, the main source of income for Poole as a port at this time were various fees charged for using the port.

Today imports include timber, steel girders, gas lines, pipes, and palletized goods; whereas, exports include clay, wheat, grain, sand, gravel and general cargo.

The markets for export and import include the Channel Islands, Europe, the Black Sea countries, North and West Africa and the Middle East.

Handling industrial cargo. Note the cruise ship in the background to the left (see Cruise Ships).

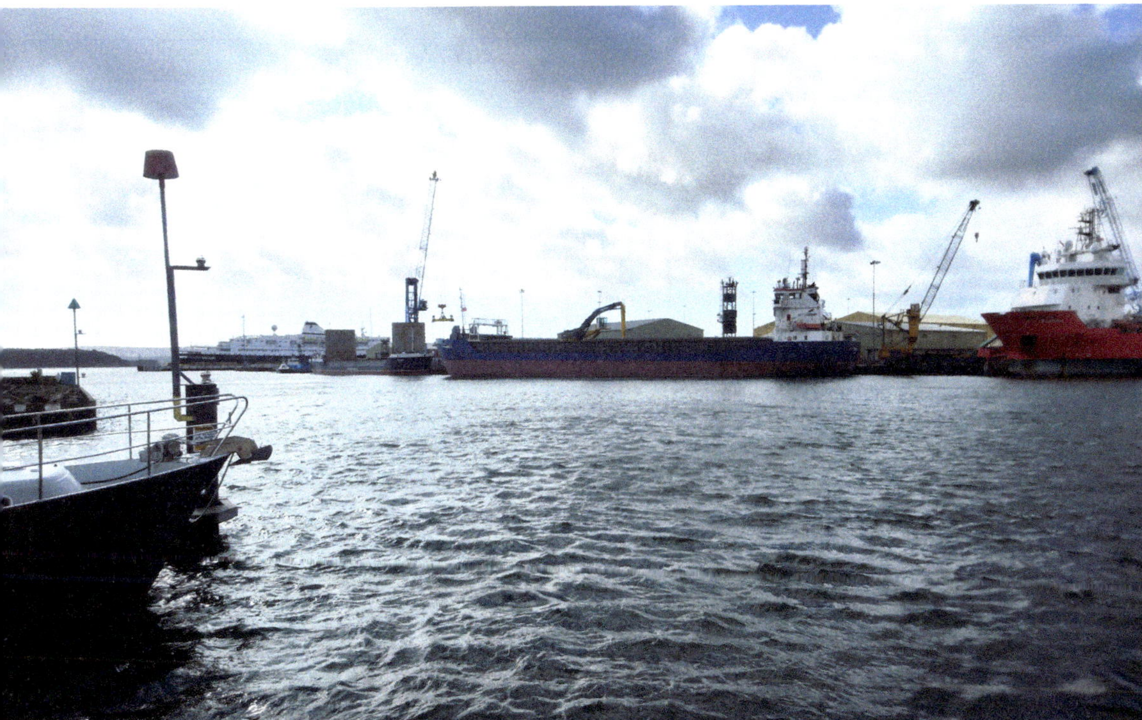

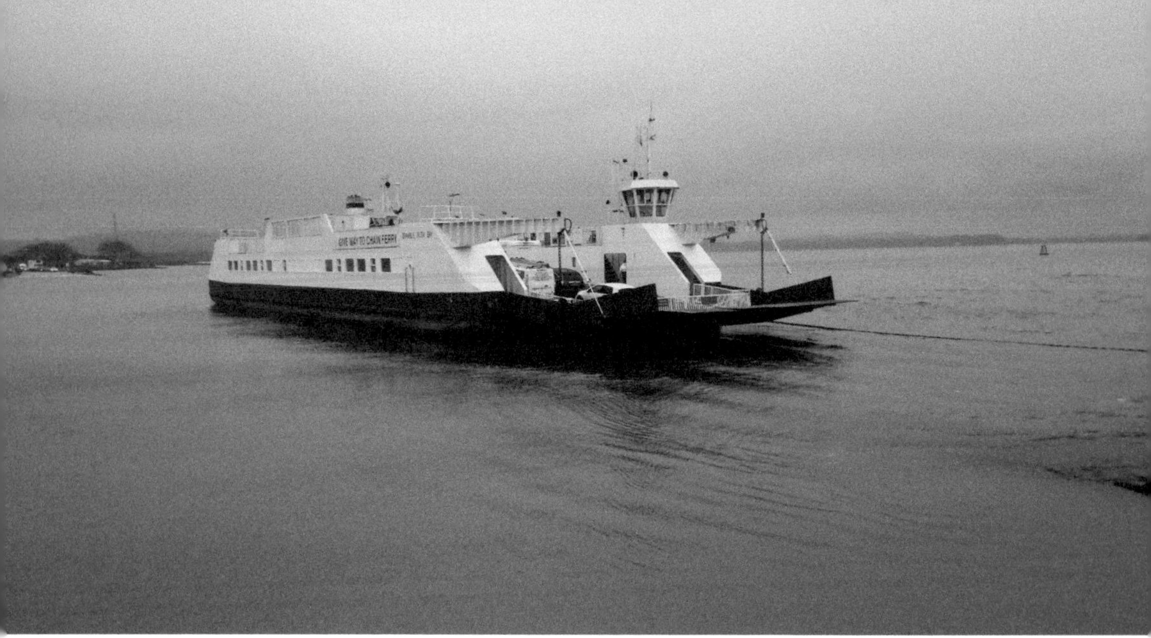

Chain ferry.

Chain Ferry

The chain ferry, which is named *Bramble Bush Bay*, plies its trade between Sandbanks and Shell Bay. This is the shortest route connecting Poole and Bournemouth to the Purbecks, and saves a detour of 25 miles.

It has a capacity of forty-eight cars, and has the right of way over all craft, apart from ships with a pilot on board.

The *Bramble Bush Bay*, which is named after a small bay near Shell Bay, is the fourth chain ferry to work this route. It is operated by Bournemouth to Swanage Motor Road and Ferry Company, and has been in service since 1994.

Coat of Arms

The Poole coat of arms features three scallop shells with a dolphin underneath, underscored by the town motto.

The scallop shell is the symbol of the Santiago Pilgrim, which has a great significance to Poole, as in the Middle Ages, many people embarked from Poole to make pilgrimages to the shrine of Saint James in Santiago de Compostela, Galicia, North West Spain. The church in the Old Town is also dedicated to Saint James.

The dolphin signifies the fishing industry, as it is considered to be the marine equivalent of the lion – a king of the seas.

The town motto, which features on the coat of arms is, 'Ad Morem Villae de Poole', which is Latin for 'according to the custom of the town of Poole'. The motto came into

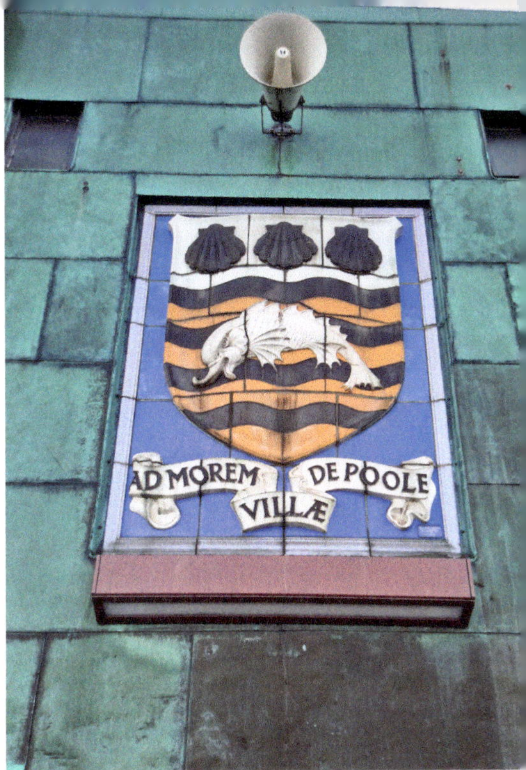

Coat of arms.

being after Queen Elizabeth I bestowed the Great Charter on Poole in 1568. In effect, Poole was granted the status of an independent county within Dorset and was styled the 'County of the Town of Poole'. This allowed Poole to own land and property, and exempted merchants from all import and export duties.

Cruise Ships

An ambitious seven-year, £10 million expansion project of South Quay has helped Poole to become a destination for cruise ships. A new 200-metre deepwater quay has been constructed to accommodate cruise and cargo ships up to 220 metres in length. This opened for business in the summer of 2018, and is one of the biggest developments seen on the south coast in recent years.

The development has enabled Poole to handle ships carrying over 1,000 passengers, as well as increasing the capacity to handle larger cargo ships. Sunseeker and other boatbuilding firms are also able to use this facility.

Custom House

The Custom House is a Georgian-style, Grade II listed building situated on the Quay.

It was granted a change of use certificate in 1995, and turned into a seafood restaurant and bar; then in 2018, it became the Custom House Café, a bistro-licensed café bar, under new ownership.

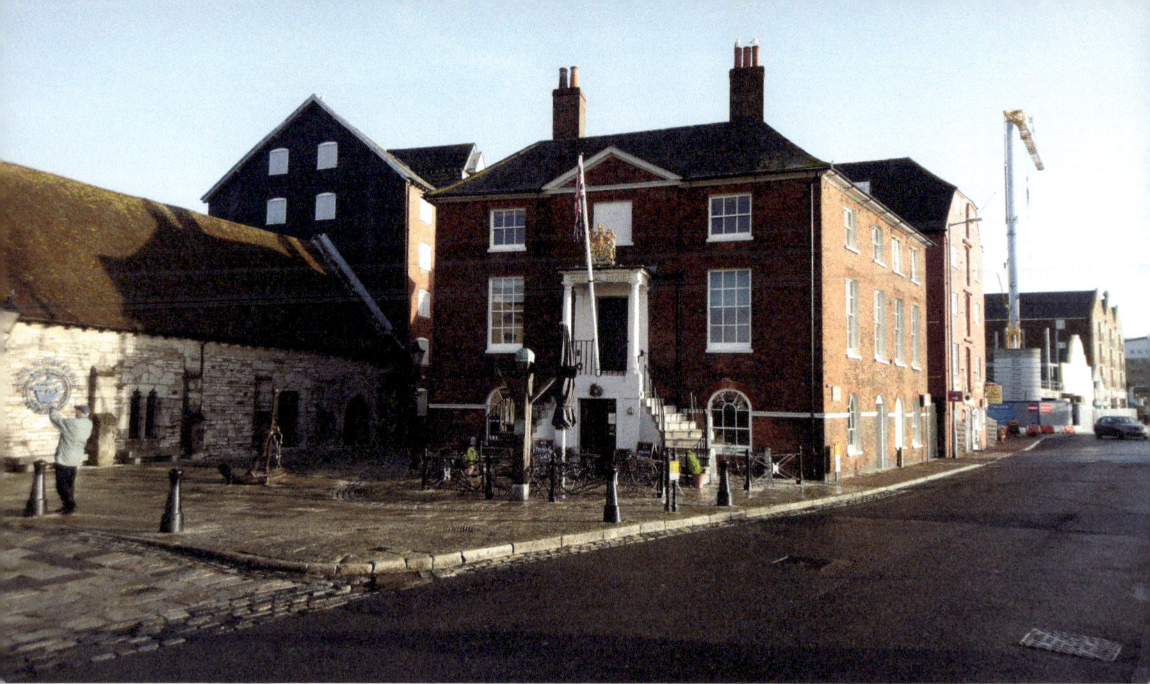

Custom House.

The original Custom House was built in 1747, but was destroyed in a fire which started nearby at the King's Arms (now The Stable) in 1813. It was rebuilt shortly afterwards, in the style of the original.

At the front of the building is a replica of a weighing beam, which was used to determine customs duty. There are also two matching flights of stairs which grandiosely sweep up to the entrance in a similar style to the steps of the Guildhall.

The Quay steps near the Custom House were known as the Custom House Steps, as this was a point where ships could berth to declare their taxable goods.

In 1747, in the same year the Custom House was built, a dramatic incident took place, in which the notorious Hawkhurst smuggling gang from the Sussex–Kent border staged a daring raid to reclaim contraband that had been confiscated by customs officials. Their vessel, named *The Three Brothers*, contained a cargo of brandy, rum, tea and coffee, and was intercepted by tidewaiters. These were customs officers who waited in customs sloops on the tide to collect duty on goods brought into a port.

The confiscated consignment was stored at the Custom House, and was guarded by a customs sloop moored alongside. Undeterred, the gang waited until low tide, which had the effect of bringing the sloop's guns below the level of the quayside, thus rendering them useless. The gang tied up the nightwatchman, before breaking in and escaping with the goods on horseback. Although, no one was injured in the original attack, a potential informer was later murdered on the roadside.

At least half of the gang were subsequently captured and hanged.

This was certainly the most audacious of the many violent attacks the Custom House has witnessed.

Dad's Army

David Croft (1922–2011) was born in Poole, and his claim to fame is co-writing with Jimmy Perry the long-running and ever-popular sitcom *Dad's Army*, about the Home Guard during the Second World War.

He drew his inspiration from his experience as a seventeen-year-old member of Poole's Home Guard, and is said to have based the gormless teenage character Pike on himself.

In order to maintain the blackout, he regularly had to tell people to turn their lights out, which fortunately he did more in the manner of Sergeant Wilson, as in: 'Would you mind awfully putting that light out', rather than, 'Turn that bloody light out', as in the more direct style of the ARP Warden Hodges.

He was actually only in the Poole Home Guard for a few months, before he was old enough to serve as a young officer in the Dorset Regiment, where he served in North Africa, India and Singapore, eventually rising to the rank of Major.

After he left the army, he worked as a Red Coat at Butlins, which provided a rich vein of material for another of his well-loved comic creations: *Hi-de-Hi!*

He then started writing pantomime scripts, before working in TV as a producer, director and writer, where he teamed up with Jimmy Perry, with whom he wrote *Dad's Army, It Ain't Half Hot Mum*, Hi-de-Hi! and *You Rang, M'Lord?* He also worked with Jeremy Lloyd, and came up with further successes: *Are You Being Served?, 'Allo 'Allo!,* and *Grace & Favour.*

Although these programmes were written decades ago, their frequent repeats bear testimony to their timeless appeal, and he deservedly received an OBE for his work in 1978.

D-Day

American troops were massing in vast numbers in Dorset from 1943 onwards in preparation for the D-Day landings, and Poole contributed greatly as the third largest embarkation point for Allied troops behind Weymouth and Portland. The vast majority of the troops were American and were destined for Omaha and Utah landing beaches in Normandy.

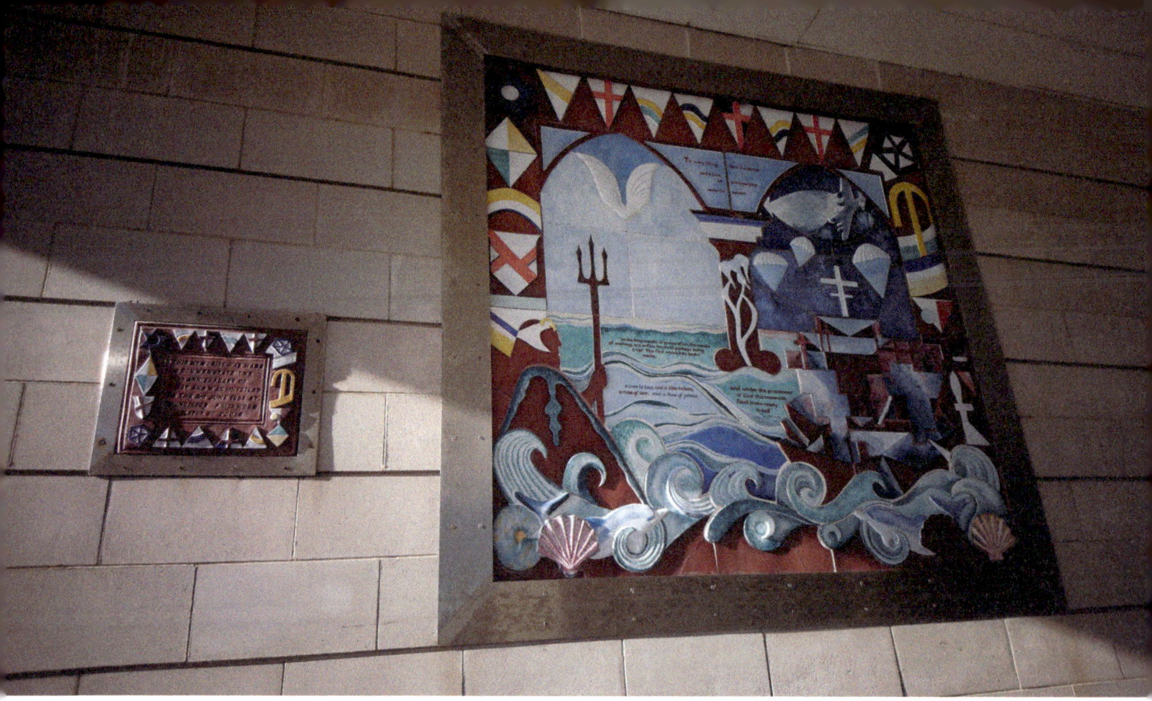

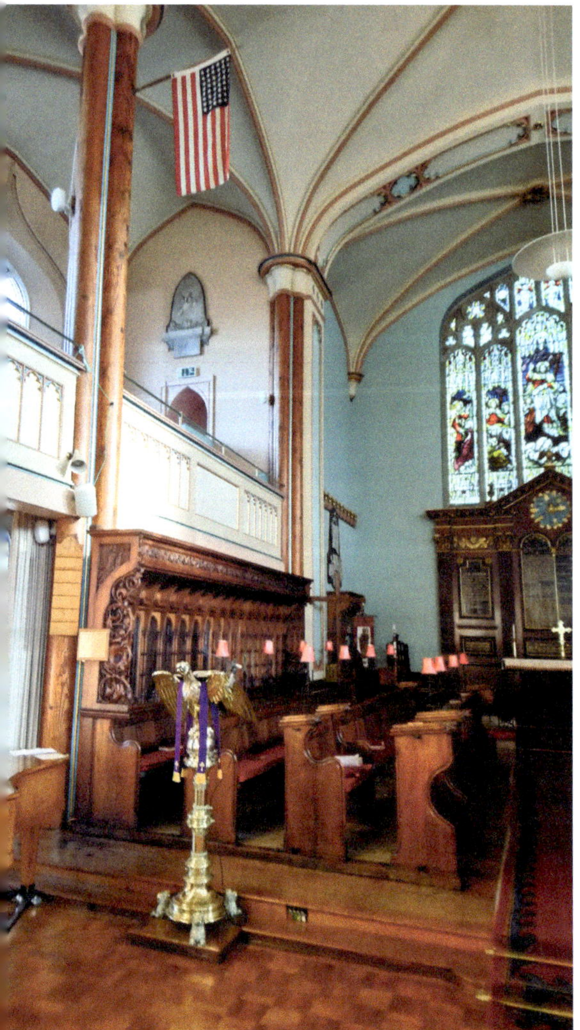

Above: A terracotta D-Day plaque created in 1994 by Poole Pottery to mark the fiftieth anniversary of D-Day.

Left: An American flag in St James' Church which flew on a US Coast Guard cutter that took part in the D-Day landings.

Below: A plaque on the Alcatraz Café, which was the Royal Navy Command Headquarters at Poole from 1940 to 1945.

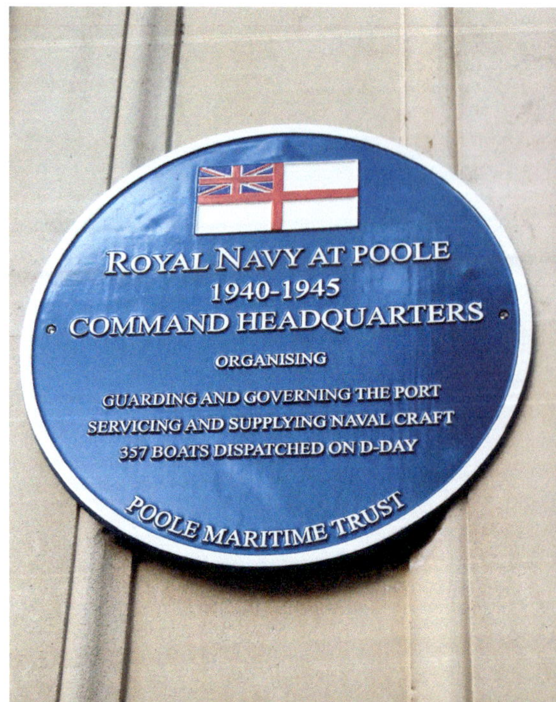

On 5 June 1944, the vanguard of 3,000 assault troops left from the Quay. They were followed in subsequent weeks by a total of 22,000 soldiers and 3,500 vessels.

Many of them perished on both beaches, but Omaha beach, forever afterwards known as 'Bloody Omaha', saw the fiercest fighting of the Allied assault on Normandy, as troops fought to secure the beachhead and the strategic Pointe du Hoc.

Local shipyards built numerous landing craft, gun boats and launches. J. Bolson and Son of Hamworthy really stepped up to the plate in the hour of need, by transforming their small yacht-building outfit into an operation that was manufacturing a landing craft per day.

Dorset Yacht Company of Hamworthy was also engaged in building landing craft, whilst other Poole/Hamworthy firms based around the Quay such as Sydenhams, Newmans, and Burt and Vick were involved in the manufacture of Mulberry Harbour, which was the temporary harbour transported across the Channel to serve as a makeshift base from which to launch the assault.

Hamworthy was a training base for troops preparing for D-Day, and had a major role in Operation Smash, a rehearsal for the real thing. This involved assaulting beaches at Studland and Shell Bay, which were both considered very similar to those in Normandy.

Disease and Pestilence

One of Dorset's least auspicious moments was the introduction of the Black Death to England.

In 1348, a sailor docked at Weymouth carrying the feared bubonic plague, which he had contracted at Gascony in France. The Black Death quickly spread throughout Weymouth before spreading right the way through England, and killing half of the population. Poole was badly affected, and it took the town a century and a half to recover.

This clump of trees was the site of the isolation hospital. Note the marshy ground at Baiter.

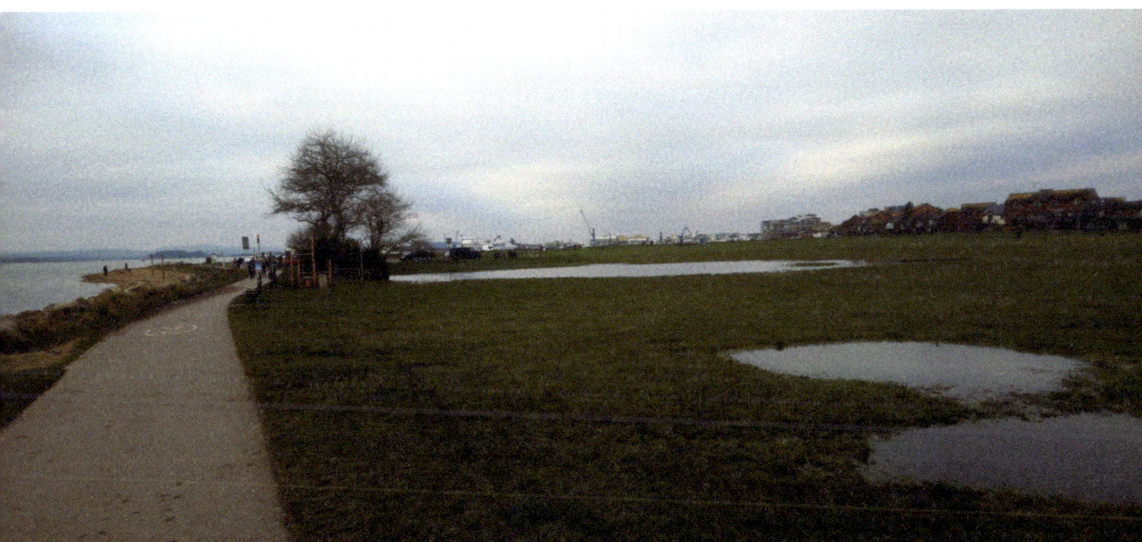

The marshy ground at Windmill Field, to the east of a former windmill, served as a burial ground for the victims. At the time, the land was a spit of land amongst open water and mudflats, and this remained the case until it was reclaimed from the sea in the 1960s, and became known as Baiter.

This area also served as a burial ground during the later plague of Britain in 1646, and it was during this period that the mayor of Poole, George Skutt, decided that isolation of the sick was necessary, and designated this spit of land to become the location of a fever hospital.

However, the hospital didn't prove large enough to house the many victims, so six further 'pest houses' were established, where people were kept in quarantine and prevented from escape by patrols of armed guards.

The same site was used again as a fever hospital in 1880 to contain a smallpox epidemic, before becoming an isolation hospital for those with infectious diseases such as smallpox, diphtheria and scarlet fever in 1893.

It then became a hospital for Royal Naval personnel during the First World War, before reverting to a hospital for infectious diseases from 1927, before finally closing in 1941.

Dolphin Centre

The Dolphin Centre is Dorset's largest indoor retail complex. It was first opened in 1969, as a two-storey shopping centre on what was called the Ladies Walking Field. It is situated at the northern end of the High Street, and was originally called the Arndale Centre.

The complex also included a sports centre (which is sadly no longer there and has been replaced by the 'Project Climbing Centre'), library, bus station and multi-storey car park.

Poole Arts Centre, Dolphin Swimming Pool and Barclays House (Barclays bank offices) were also built shortly afterwards – apparently they are all fine examples of late sixties and early seventies architecture, so are listed buildings and can't be pulled down, despite them being square-block monstrosities; the type of thing that would give Prince Charles nightmares.

The Arndale Centre was hugely popular with children as it featured wooden sculptured animals to climb on.

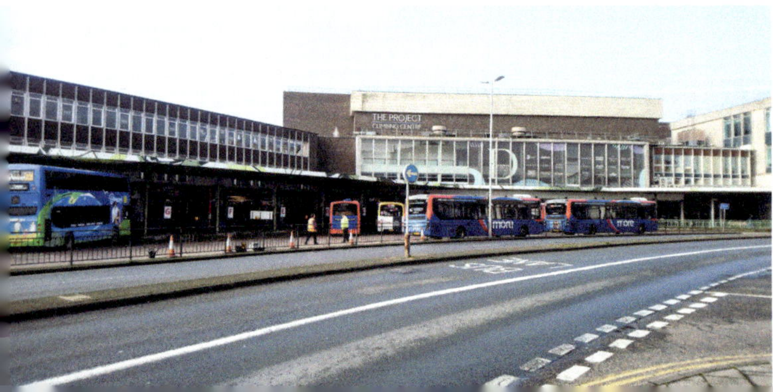

The Dolphin Centre. Not all of Poole is a beautiful place.

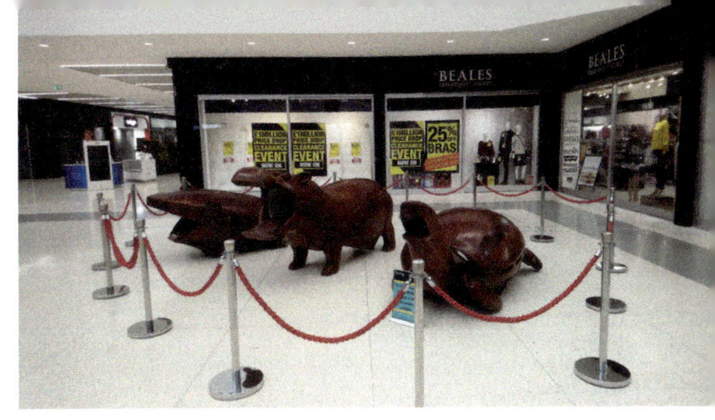

These wooden animals appeared in 2019 as an exhibition celebrating fifty years of the shopping centre. They are much smaller than the originals, which were large enough to accommodate many children climbing in and out of them.

In 1988, a revamp took place, and the Arndale Centre was renamed the Dolphin Centre, and Poole High Street became pedestrianised in order to link the High Street to the shopping centre more easily. However, the wooden animals were retained until 1997.

There are proposals afoot to further refurbish the Dolphin Centre and incorporate a seven-screen multiplex cinema.

Dream Machine Bike Night

On Tuesday nights between April and September, motorcycle enthusiasts come from far and wide to Britain's largest weekly bike night. They come to meet fellow enthusiasts for a beer and a chat and of course to show off their pride and joy.

The Quay is closed to cars, as it becomes a sea of gleaming paintwork and chrome, and a cacophony of throbbing engine noise. There is also a second arena at Harbourside Park, just a bit further along the shore from the Quay, for those frequent occasions when the quay is overly full with bikes.

The event has become popular with bikers, non-biking locals and tourists alike.

Dream Machine Bike Night.

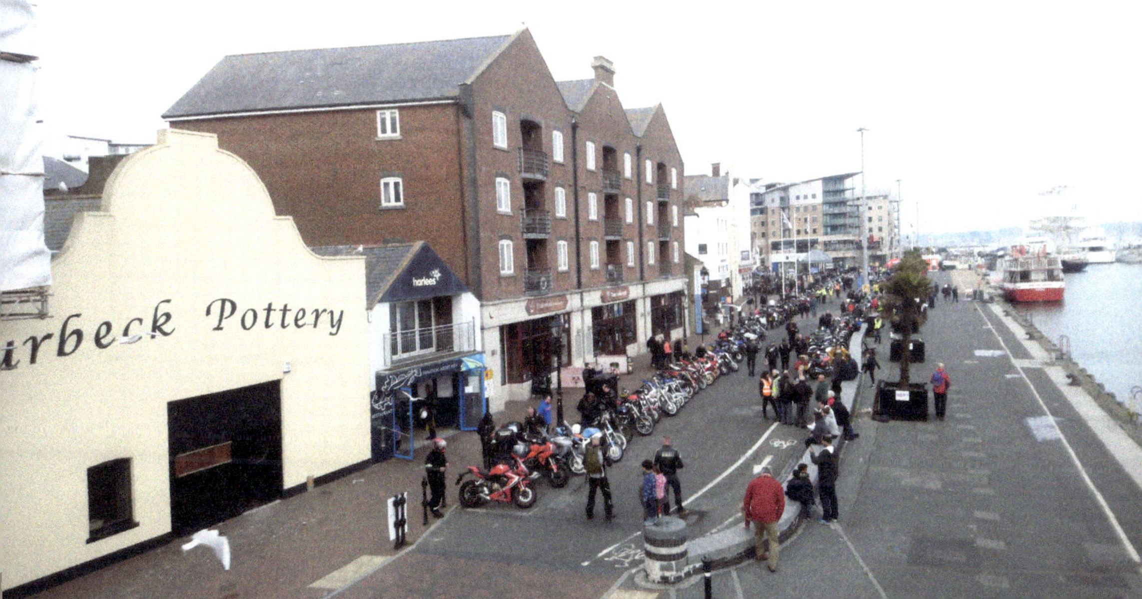

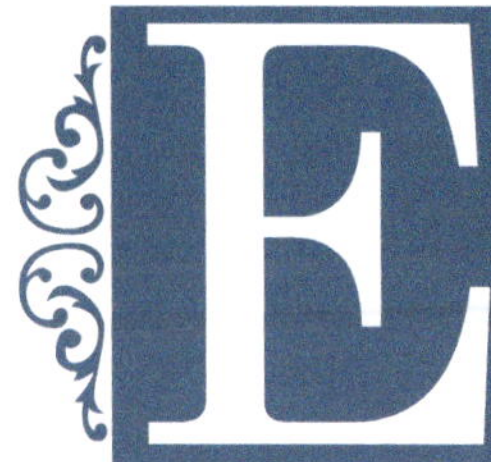

Execution Site

The Poole gallows was situated in the area now known as Baiter, to the west of what was Windmill Field at Windmill Point. A vast open space was required due to the large crowds that were usually attracted.

They were first used in the fourteenth century, but had a good airing during the Judge Jeffreys-led Bloody Assizes following the Monmouth Rebellion of 1685.

The Bloody Assizes were savage and barbaric. There was no leniency, as adults of either sex, or children as young as ten or twelve, were beheaded or transported.

Those involved in the rebellion were sentenced for High Treason for which the penalty was death. In the case of a commoner, the method of execution was to be hanged drawn and quartered. This involved being fastened to a hurdle and dragged by a horse to the place of execution, where he was then hanged almost to the point of death. The victim then had his genitals cut off, before being slit from the breastbone to the groin, whereupon his entrails were pulled out, and then burnt in front of him. Next, he was beheaded, and then quartered – chopped into four pieces. The pieces were then put on public display in prominent places.

For reasons of public decency, the punishment for High Treason for women was to be burnt at the stake.

The executioners at Dorchester, where the Bloody Assizes took place, were struggling, as so many were convicted of High Treason. They complained that they could only cope with thirteen of these a day, as the process was pretty time-consuming. As a result, gallows were also erected at Bridport, Weymouth, Poole and Wareham, as the condemned were farmed out in batches to the various locations. Twelve of the miscreants were hanged on Monmouth Beach, Lyme Regis, at the site of the original invasion.

Alan Skutt, who was mayor of Poole at the time, was responsible for sending the quarters out to local villages to be displayed prominently in gibbets. These were iron cages used to display the body parts, which were tarred to make them last longer, and then left as a grim reminder to cower the local people.

Records of hangings are a little sketchy, but there is a record of a further two hangings at Windmill Point in 1736.

Later in 1752, Anthony Colpis and his wife were accused of throwing an elderly widow out of a third-floor window and causing her death. Mrs Colpis was acquitted but her husband was hanged at Windmill Point.

The last hanging at this location took place in 1759.

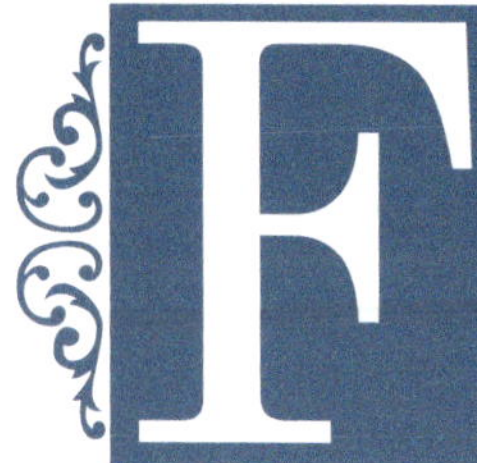

Ferries

In 1974, the Truckline service was inaugurated to transport lorries and their cargoes to and from Cherbourg, France. This led, in 1977, to Poole becoming twinned with Cherbourg.

Later, Brittany Ferries introduced a passenger ferry, the *Barfleur*, which operates a daily scheduled service to Cherbourg, and then also introduced a freight line to Bilbao, Spain.

Meanwhile a high-speed ferry, the *Condor Express*, was established, which runs services to Jersey and Guernsey, as well as St Malo in Brittany, France.

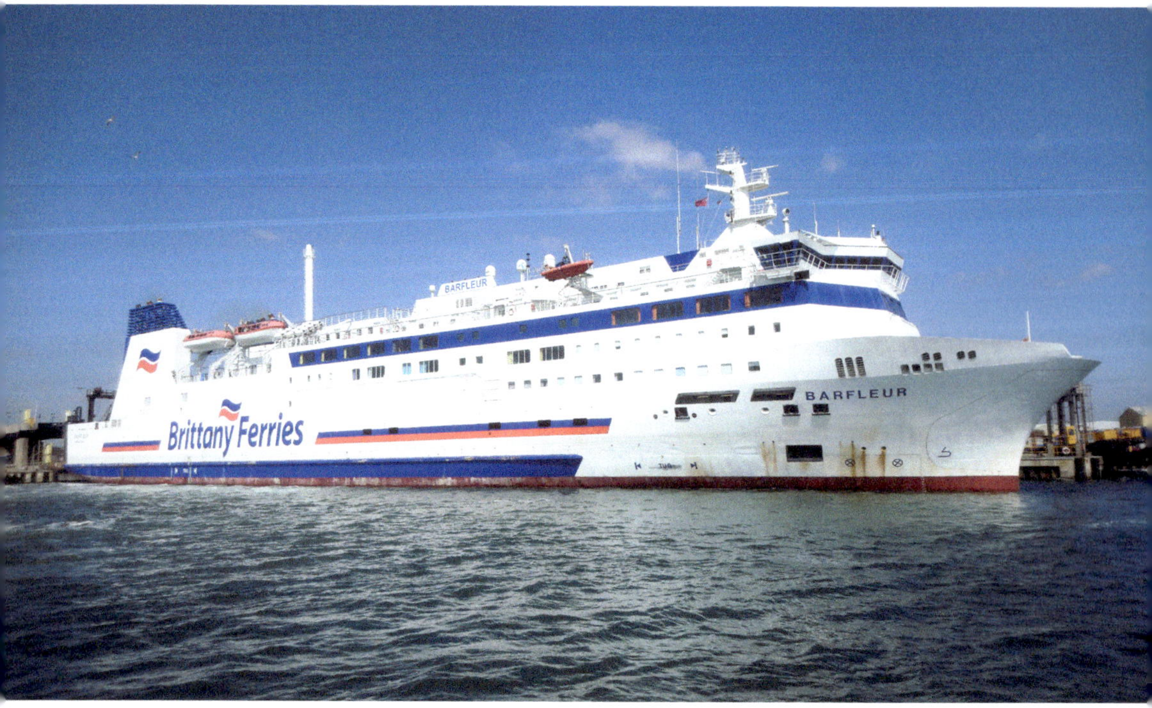

The *Barfleur*.

Fishing

Around 300 commercial fishing boats operate out of Dorset ports, and the fishing industry is a key facet of the region.

The town of Poole was built on fishing, and there is still a sizeable fleet consisting of around 100 registered boats, based at Fishermen's Dock.

The shallow harbour is a significant breeding ground for mussels, clams, oysters and cockles, so the fishing fleet mainly focuses on shellfish and crustaceans from within the Harbour, although, many also venture further afield into the English Channel to catch crustaceans or other fish such as mackerel, plaice, cod and various flat fish.

Some of the world's finest oysters are bred in Poole Harbour, and a ready market is found among the numerous hotels and restaurants of this part of the world, as well as in China and Japan.

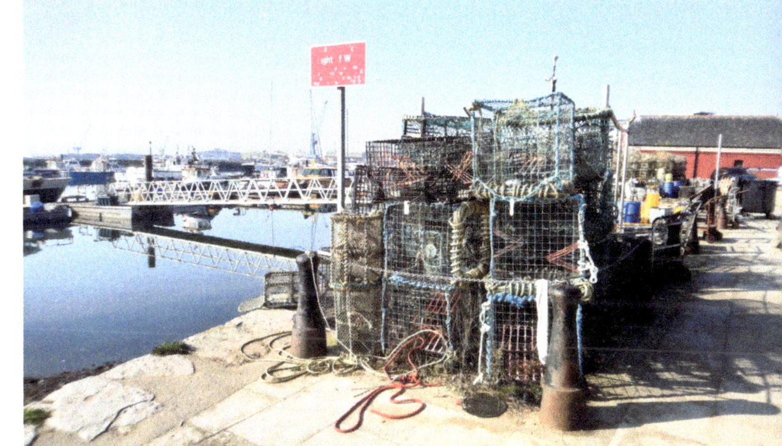

Right: Fishermen's Pots at Fishermen's Dock.

Below: Fishing fleet.

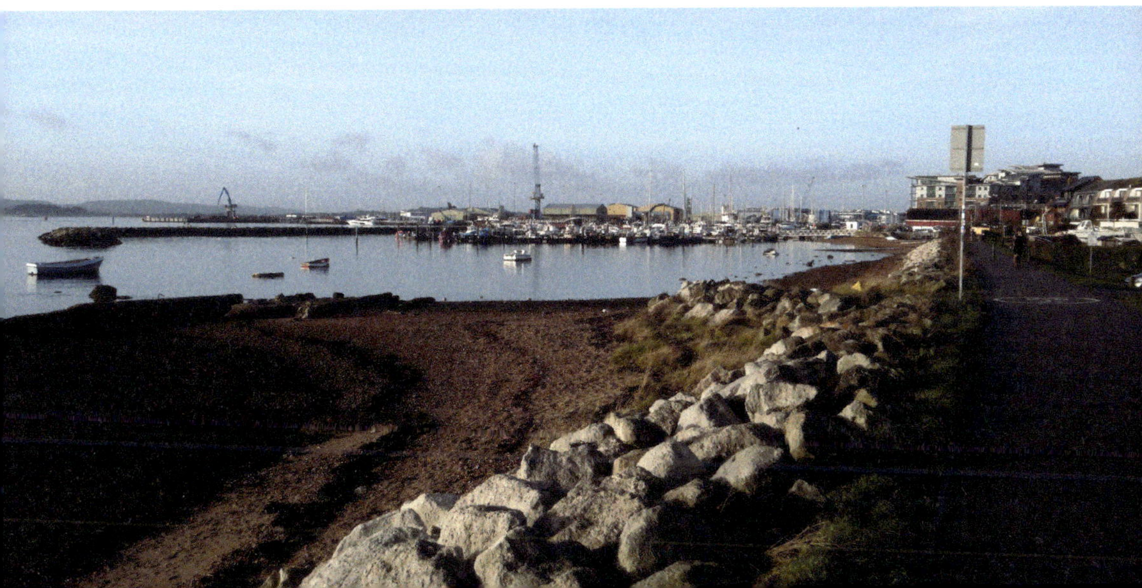

Flying Boats

Salterns Hotel is situated adjacent to a 285-berth marina. The hotel incorporates a bar and restaurant, which has a large seating area outside providing pleasant views of the marina and harbour.

In the eighteenth century, the area was active in the production of salt, and was originally called Salterns, but later changed to Lilliput. Some say the change of name was due to the connection with the smuggler Isaac Gulliver (see Smugglers – Gulliver, Isaac).

Prior to the Second World War, Salterns was the location of a dockyard for a pottery firm, before becoming the Harbour Yacht Hotel. However, during the Second World War, the site was the British Overseas Airways Corporation (BOAC) terminal for civil passenger flying boat operations. There were also military flying boat stations variously located at other points around the Quay; the main one being RAF Hamworthy.

At this time, Salterns was Britain's only international airport and famous passengers have included royalty, test cricketers, various film stars and politicians, including Winston Churchill.

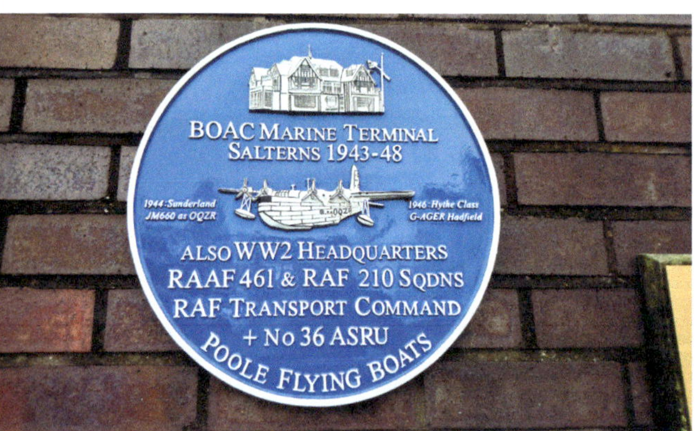

Left: A plaque relating to the flying boats at Salterns Hotel.

Below: Salterns Hotel.

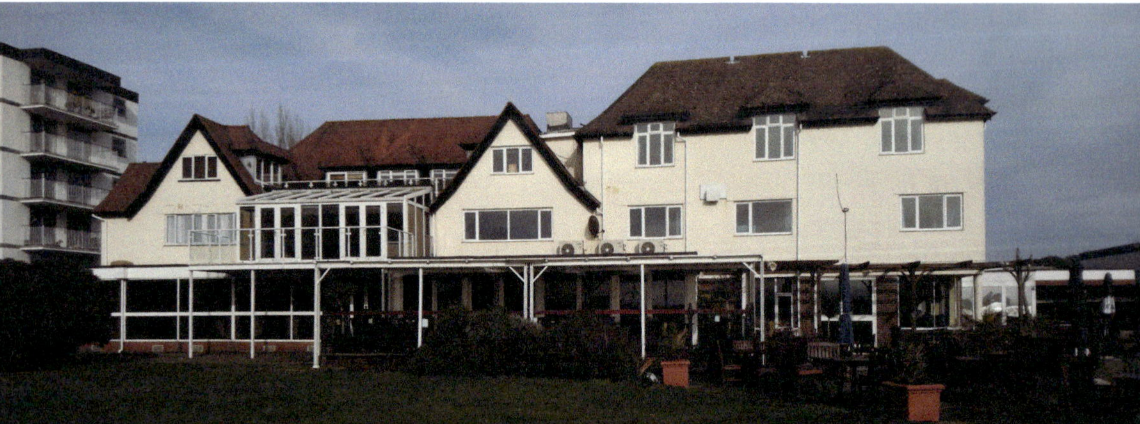

After the war, it returned to its former use as a marina, and Poole Harbour Yacht Club took over.

The sea wall of the marina was created using remnants of the D-Day Mulberry Harbour (see D-Day), which was built in Poole.

British Overseas Airways Corporation (BOAC), Poole

As early as 1938, when war was imminent, Salterns was earmarked as a base to move flying boat operations to, as Poole was considered less likely to be on the receiving end of heavy bombing than the original base at Southampton.

British Overseas Airways Corporation (BOAC) was formed by the merger of Imperial Airways and British Airways in 1939, and in early 1940, flights from Salterns began in earnest.

On 3 August 1940, the first flight across the Atlantic by a British Commercial Airline was a BOAC flying boat passenger flight which took off from Salterns.

They also flew to Australia, and flights from Poole to Sydney could take five–seven days depending on the weather.

Throughout the war and until 1948, BOAC had 600 staff in Poole to support their various flight crews and flying boat services.

In addition to Salterns, other premises were requisitioned at Poole Pottery and on the Quay to provide backup services, such as administration and cargo storage.

The flying boats were moored in the water and passengers, mail and freight were ferried to them from launches. The flying boats then took off from the water. There were twelve high-speed launches, with sixty staff operating them.

Today Poole is recognised as the birthplace of BOAC and the forerunner of British Airways, although, after the war the flying boats returned to Hythe in Southampton.

RAF Hamworthy

461 Squadron
The base for military flying boats was at RAF Hamworthy, which was rapidly constructed, and then commissioned in 1942. It became the base for 461 Squadron Royal Australian Air Force, known as the ANZAC squadron. There was a staff of 300 including crew and engineers.

The base didn't have any hangars for the aircraft, so maintenance had to be carried out on the hard standing.

In May 1943, 461 Squadron were transferred out. During their stay, eighty-three personnel lost their lives. Their bravery and exploits are still remembered both in Poole and in Australia.

210 Squadron

In 1943, 461 Squadron were replaced at RAF Hamworthy by 210 Squadron. They became known as the Catalina Squadron due to their fleet of twelve American-built Catalina flying boats. They consisted of forty-six officers, 235 other ranks and twenty-one WAAFs (Women's Auxiliary Air Force). They continued the vital work of their predecessors in spotting and sinking enemy U-boats.

One of the officers, John Cruickshank, was awarded a Victoria Cross. He was badly injured when sinking a U-boat in the Arctic, but then managed to pilot his badly damaged flying boat to the safe haven of the Shetlands.

In early 1944, 210 Squadron were moved out, as RAF Hamworthy transferred to the Royal Navy and became HMS *Turtle* in the build-up to D-Day (see D-Day).

After D-Day it became a Royal Marines base (see Royal Marines).

Royal Navy Air Station Sandbanks

765 Squadron

In July 1940, the Royal Motor Yacht Club at Sandbanks became RNAS Sandbanks, and home to Squadron 765 of the Royal Navy Fleet Air Arm relocated from Lee on Solent. It had responsibility for seaplane training and air sea rescue for the area.

RNAS Sandbanks had twelve seaplanes and 100 personnel, but in the run-up to D-Day, 765 Squadron was disbanded.

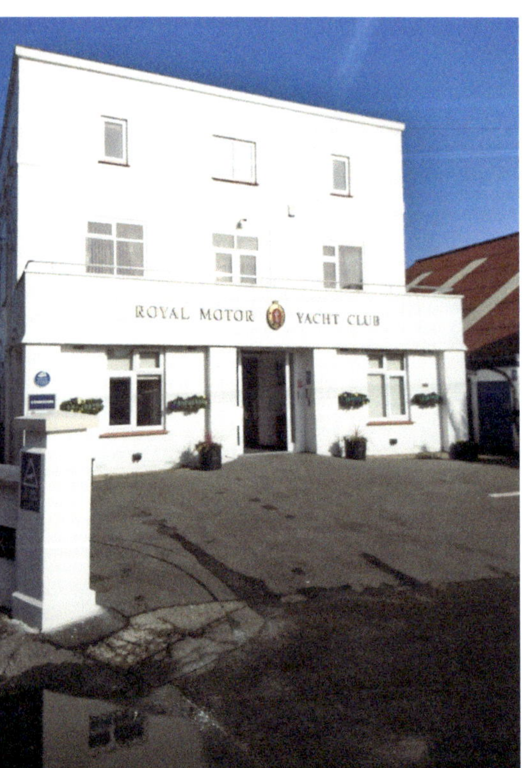

Left: The Royal Motor Yacht Club at Sandbanks became the Royal Navy Air Station Sandbanks during the Second World War.

Below: A plaque at the Royal Motor Yacht Club.

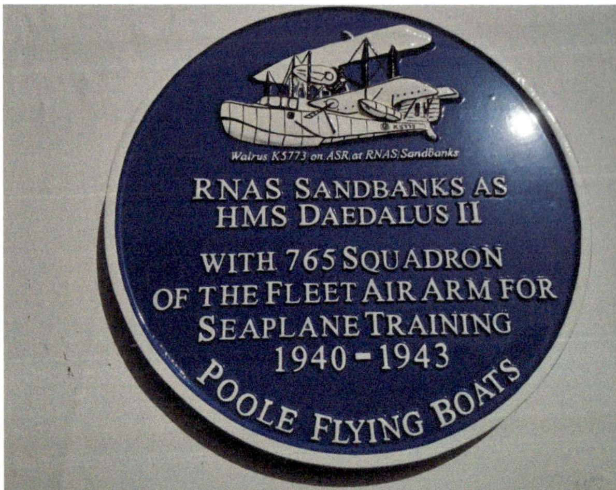

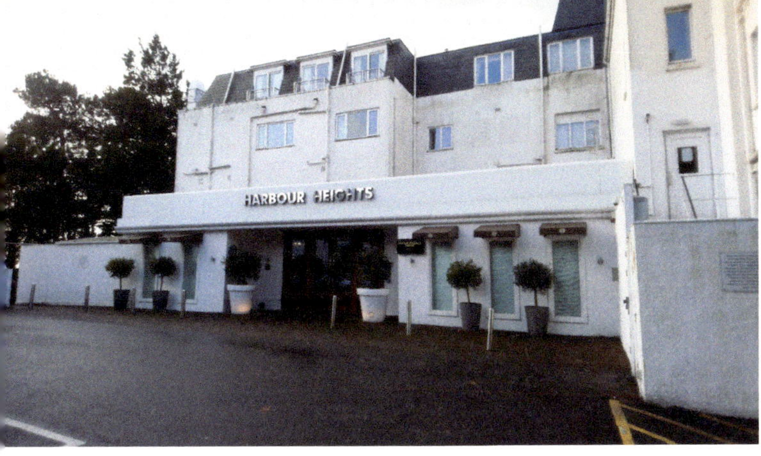

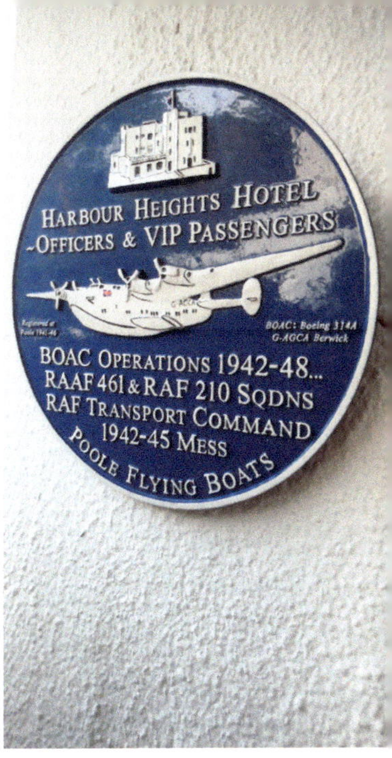

Above: Harbour Heights Hotel.

Right: A plaque at the Harbour Heights Hotel.

Today, the Royal Motor Yacht Club, along with the boat shed that was used for the flying boats provide a poignant reminder of those times.

The Harbour Heights Hotel was also requisitioned for use as a mess for the squadron officers.

Football (Poole Town FC)

Poole Town FC was formed in 1890, after the amalgamation of Poole Rovers and Poole Hornets. They initially played at Fernside Road, which was then called Breakheart Lane, and turned semi-professional in 1926.

That season also saw their best-ever run in the FA Cup, reaching the third round, where they lost to Everton at Goodison Park.

In 1933 they moved into Poole Stadium, owned by Poole Borough Council, which they initially shared with Poole Cycling Club, who used the track around the outside of the

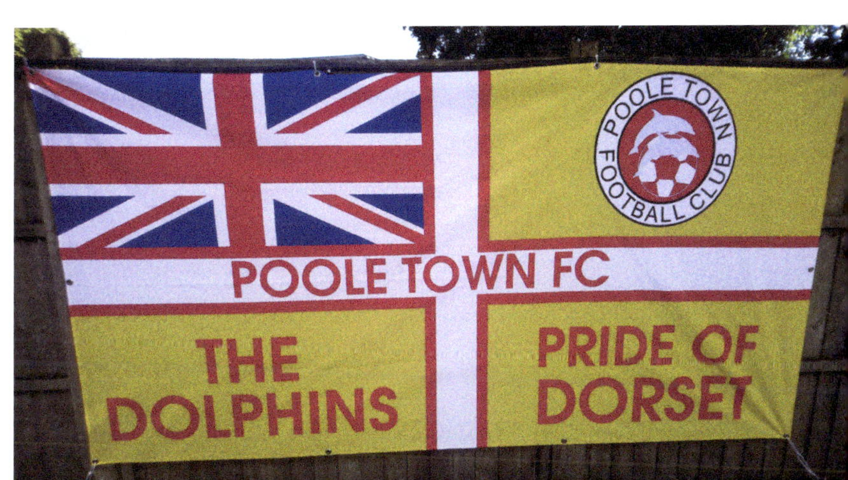

Poole Town
FC flag.

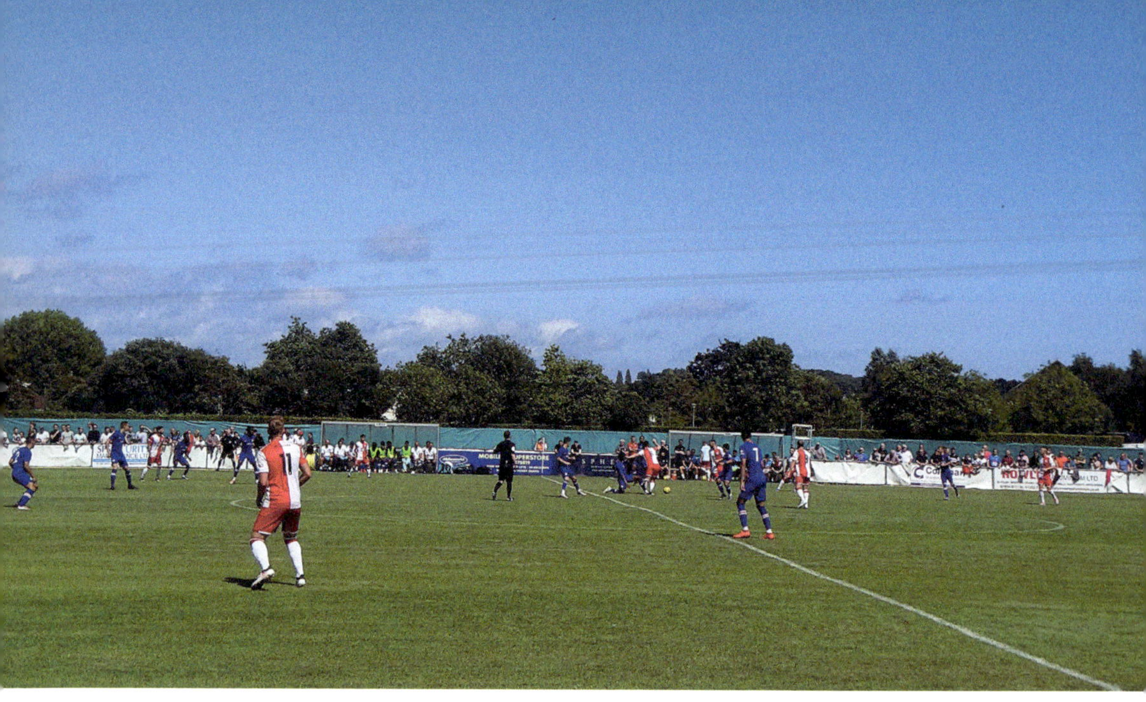

Poole Town in action against a Chelsea XI (naturally none of their superstars were included) in a pre-season friendly before the 2019/20 season. Fans of the TV show *Love Island* may recognise the man on the ball as Marvin Brooks who featured in the 2019 version.

pitch. Then in 1948, Poole Pirates Motorcycle Speedway team and Poole Greyhound Racing moved in to the stadium.

However, in 1994, Poole Borough Council forced the football club to leave citing low attendances. This coincided with the widening of the greyhound track, meaning that the football pitch in the middle of the track no longer met the regulation dimensions, so Poole Town FC were obliged to move elsewhere.

This was particularly galling for the club, as during their stay at the stadium, they had financed various ground improvements including a 1,000-seat grandstand and covered terracing on the western side in 1960.

After moving, they initially shared a ground with Hamworthy United, before moving to their current Tatnam Ground.

The ground situation has held the club back over many years, as they have frequently missed out on promotions due to inadequate facilities. However, in the 2015/16 season they achieved promotion to the Nationwide League South, and after ground improvements were allowed to take their place in the highest league in their history.

However, the following season would have seen Poole Town in the play-offs to gain further promotion; but yet again, their facilities let them down and they were denied their rightful play-off place due to an inadequate amount of seating.

They were relegated in the 2017/18 season, and currently reside in the Bet Victor Southern Premier South League, which is three tiers away from the actual Football League.

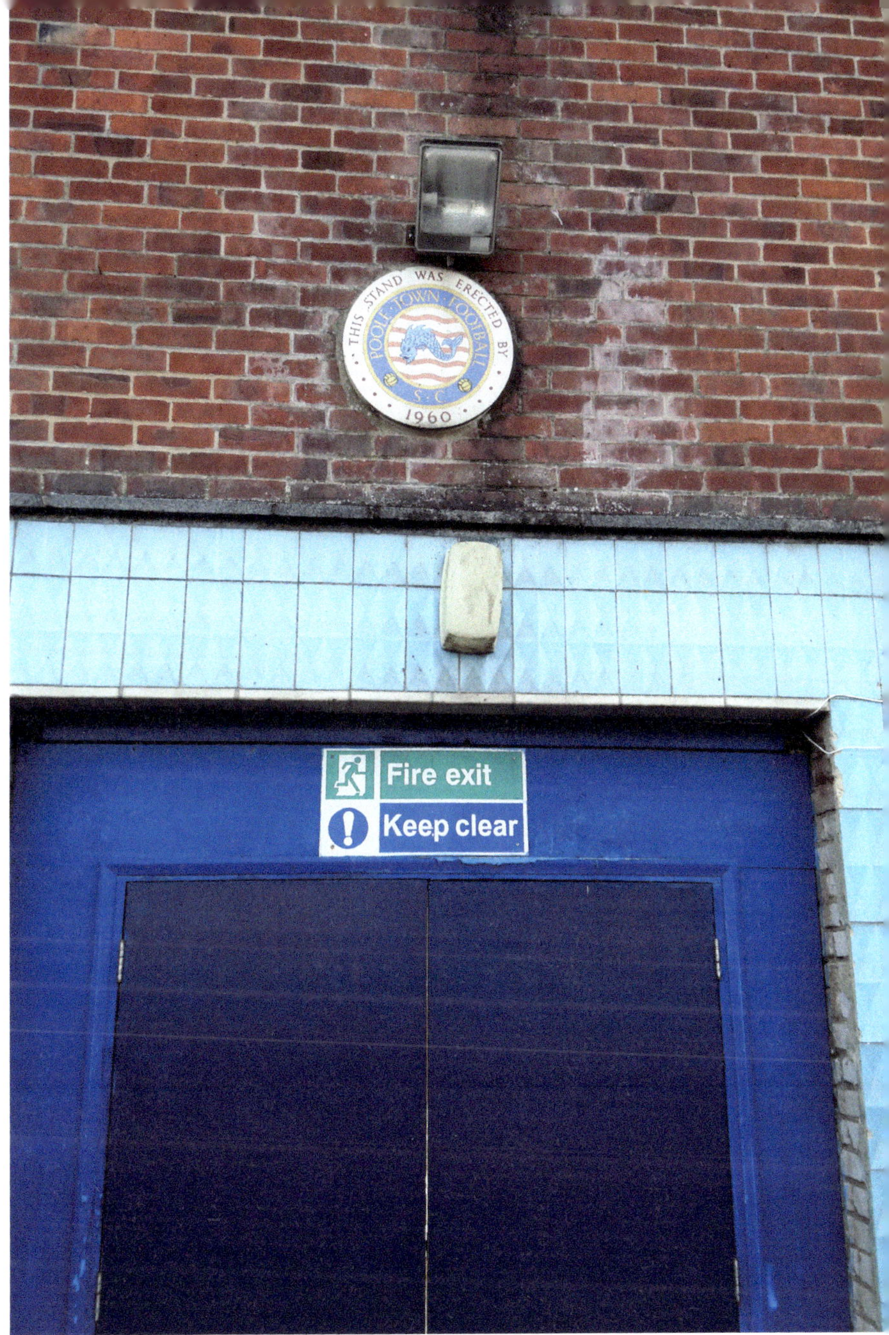

A plaque erected at Poole Stadium in recognition of the stand financed by Poole Town FC in 1960.

However, they are a thriving club within the community at all levels, with no fewer than thirty-two youth teams, an Under 18s Development Squad, two ladies' teams, a walking football team and a Disability Counts team.

One of their best-known prodigies is Charlie Austin, who has since played for Swindon Town, Burnley, Queens Park Rangers, Southampton and West Bromwich Albion. He was also picked for an England squad in 2015, but didn't feature on the pitch.

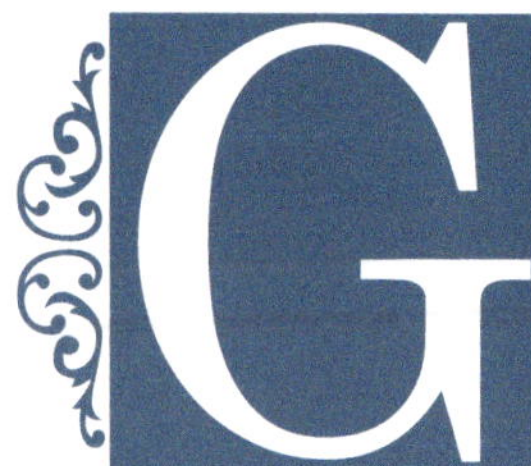

Granny Cousins

Poole's last 'knocker upper', was Granny Cousins, who operated in late Victorian and early Edwardian times between the Quay and the gasworks. Her job was to rouse the ropewalk workers and the factory workers in the early hours, by tapping on their windows with a long pole.

She then went to her main employment, which was working on the ropewalk. Ropewalk workers were those involved in making ropes primarily for sailing ships, or Royal Naval vessels, for which around 30 miles of rope would be required.

They worked in dusty, dirty, sweatshop conditions, as they weaved long strands of hemp into ropes. They also had to contend with frequent outbreaks of fire as the friction of the weaving process often caused the hemp to catch alight.

Tourist's can now go on Granny Cousins Ghost Walk tours to learn of the history of Poole and those who haunt the town.

Guildhall

The Guildhall is one of Poole's most historic and iconic buildings, and is Grade II listed. It was built in 1761 by Poole's two Members of Parliament, as a symbol of the town's affluence.

The prosperity was due to trade with Newfoundland (see Newfoundland Trade), and many of Poole's great merchant families such as the Lesters, the Garlands and the Jolliffes were building themselves impressive Georgian mansions, many of which still predominate in the merchants quarter of the Old Town, around St James' Church.

The Guildhall looks similar in appearance to the old Custom House, as they are both characterised by ostentatious dual staircases.

In the seventeenth century, the Guildhall came to symbolise power and trade. It was a meeting place for Poole's councilors, and there was a police station next door. It was also used as a courtroom, where sentences of public floggings or transportation would frequently be dished out to the unfortunate miscreants.

The ground floor, which is now enclosed, used to consist of open-fronted market stalls, and was used twice weekly as a meat market.

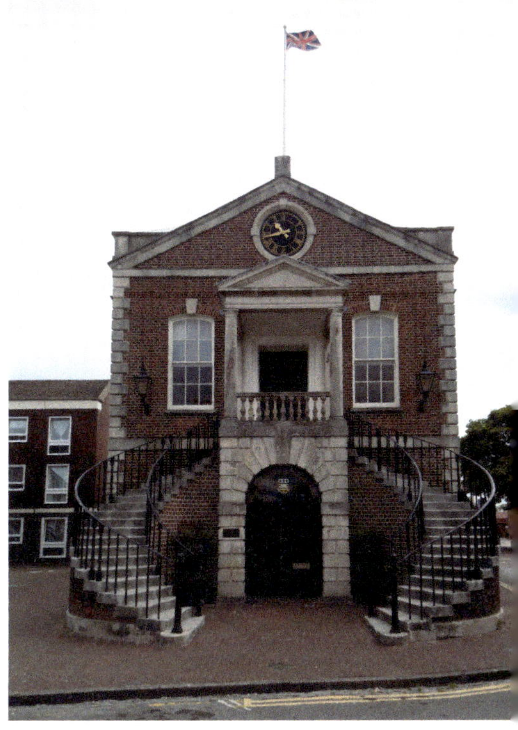

The Guildhall.

In 1815, after the Battle of Waterloo brought an end to the Napoleonic Wars, the Newfoundland trade collapsed and the town lost its prosperity. During this time, the Guildhall was pressed into service as the parish church, as St James'; the church in the Old Town had been pulled down in 1819, in order to be rebuilt.

In 1885, political reform resulted in town clerk, Robert Parr, being made redundant. He subsequently made an outrageous compensation claim, which the High Court ordered the Guildhall to pay. The Guildhall tried to increase the rates in order to meet the bill, but was met with a flat refusal from the householders. Consequently, the Guildhall was unable to settle the claim, and the High Court ruled that the Guildhall had to be handed over to Mr Parr as payment.

Robert Parr was obviously a very bitter man, as to rub salt into the wounds he rented the Guildhall to a farmer who kept cattle in it. Meanwhile the council were unable to feed the poor, or buy gas for the street lights.

In 1944, the Guildhall became a kind of NAAFI – i.e. a canteen and meeting room for American servicemen preparing for D-Day, and was also used as washrooms.

After the war, the washing facilities were left in place, for use by local people living in the tenements, where washing facilities were virtually nonexistent. These replaced the previous slipper baths (a place where people could wash), which had been flattened by the Luftwaffe. This usage of the Guildhall was only discontinued in the 1960s, after the slum clearances (see Slum Clearances).

After the war, it was used as an art school, and then in the 1960s, it housed Poole Museum, before the museum moved to its current site on the Quay in 1991.

The Guildhall was unused and falling into a state of disrepair between 1991 and 2007, until the rules governing civil marriages were altered, meaning it could be put to good use once again, as the Borough of Poole's Register Office.

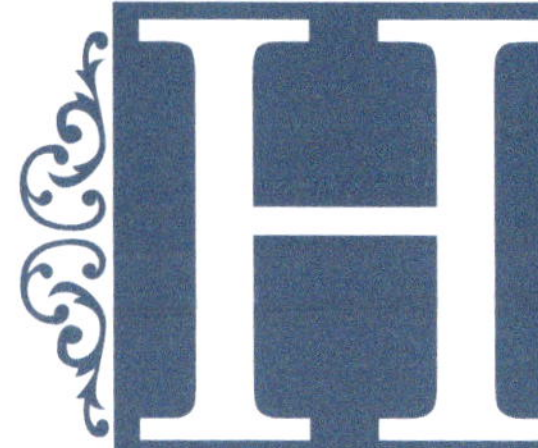

Hamilton, Horatio

Bullet marks can be seen in the wall of the Guildhall which date back to a murder that took place in May 1886, when local man John King was drowning his sorrows in the Angel public house next door.

The recent death of King's father had left him as the sole breadwinner, supporting his mother and sisters. His father had been a harbour pilot, and John King wished to continue in that role using his father's boat. However, he was persistently refused a permit by Alderman Horatio Hamilton, who claimed the boat was unseaworthy.

When Alderman Hamilton made an appearance on the Guildhall steps, King rushed out of the pub to confront him, and after a heated discussion, launched a salvo of shots at him.

He was initially sentenced to hang, but an angry reaction from those in Poole who sympathized with his plight meant that he was sent to a lunatic asylum instead.

Angel and Guildhall.

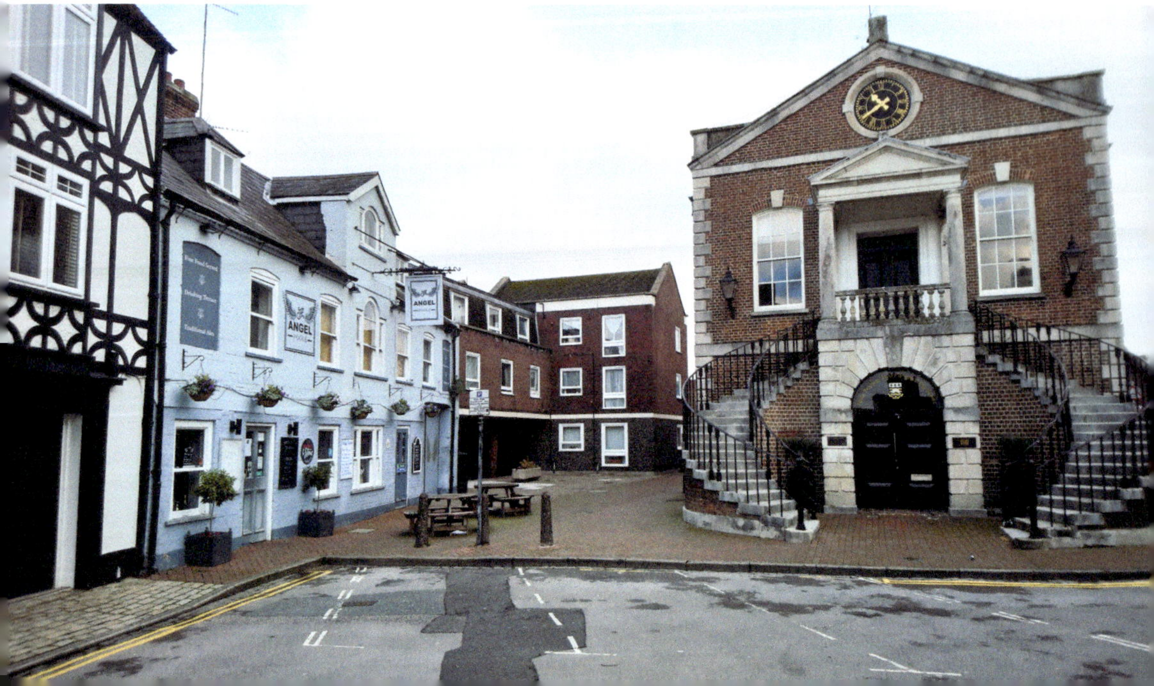

Harbour Office

At the junction of Thames Street and the Quay, adjoining the King's Hall part of the King Charles, and fronting onto the Quay opposite the entrance of the Custom House, is the Harbour Office. It was built in 1727 as a reading room for ships' captains and town merchants and is now used by the coastguard.

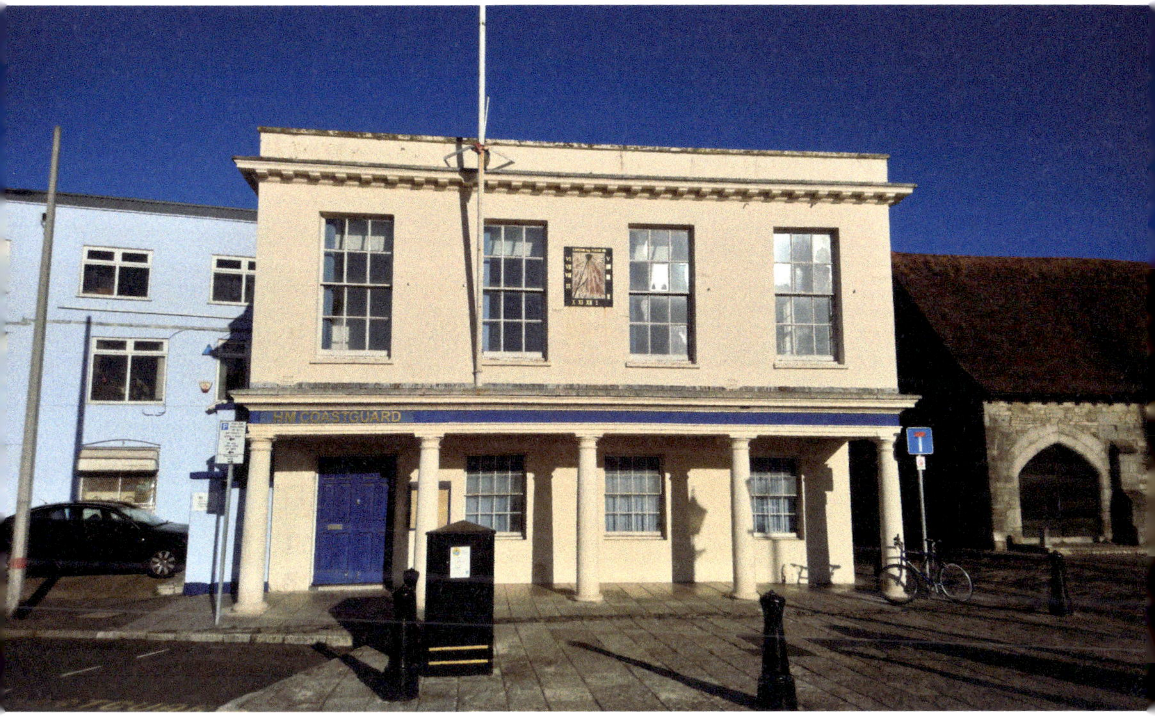

Above: Harbour Office.

Right: Relief stone carving of Benjamin Skutt.

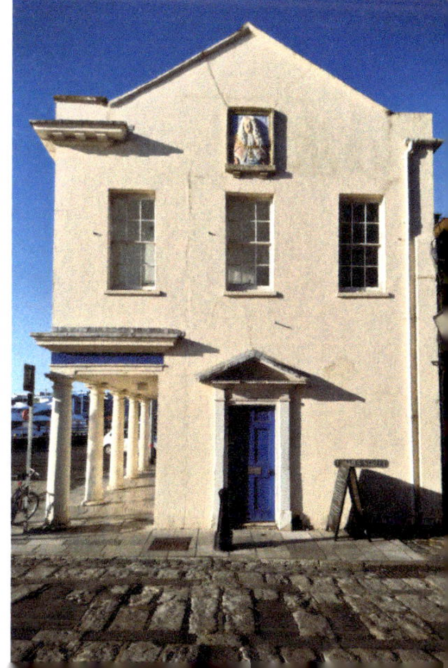

On the front of the building facing the Quay there is a sundial which is dedicated to S. Weston, mayor of Poole in 1814. On a side wall is a relief stone carving of Benjamin Skutt, mayor of Poole on three occasions – 1717, 1727 and 1742.

Hero of Dunkirk

The lifeboat which now takes centre stage in the Lifeboat Museum, at the site of the old lifeboat station, played a heroic role in the Dunkirk evacuation of 30 May 1940.

Thomas Kirk Wright was built in 1938 and is now one of only two surviving surf-class lifeboats. She was Poole's first motorised lifeboat.

On the first day of the evacuation, she was the first lifeboat to make it to Dunkirk. She made three trips over four days, rescuing many troops. On the final return journey, she was loaded with French troops and came under heavy fire, which caused widespread damage to the boat. Although, no one was hit, she had to limp home on only one engine.

After extensive repairs she returned to lifeboat duty in Poole, before retiring in 1962.

Hotel du Vin

The Grade II listed building, which is now the Hotel du Vin, was first commissioned by the successful Newfoundland merchant Isaac Lester in 1776, and then completed by his brother Benjamin.

Isaac and Benjamin Lester were part of an important merchant family that were running Poole's largest Newfoundland fishing and trading outfit and accumulating great wealth as a result.

The Port and Starboard Conference Room, which was formerly known as the Lester-Garland Room, houses a marble fireplace, which is adorned, appropriately enough, with two marble cod fillets.

George Garland was a Newfoundland trader who achieved success by developing close trading relationships with the Newfoundland settlements, and also by fostering further close relationships by marrying Benjamin Lester's daughter.

Benjamin Lester was the Member of Parliament for Poole from 1790 to 1796, and later George Garland followed suit, becoming the Member of Parliament for Poole from 1801 to 1806, as well as being mayor of Poole on two occasions.

George Garland inherited the Lester's Newfoundland business, and his son John Bingley Garland also became mayor of Poole.

In the 1960s the premises became the Mansion House, which was initially licensed as a dining establishment for members only, but then expanded to become a non-members' restaurant and hotel.

The Mansion House was taken over by the national chain Hotel du Vin in 2007, and is now a hotel, restaurant and bar.

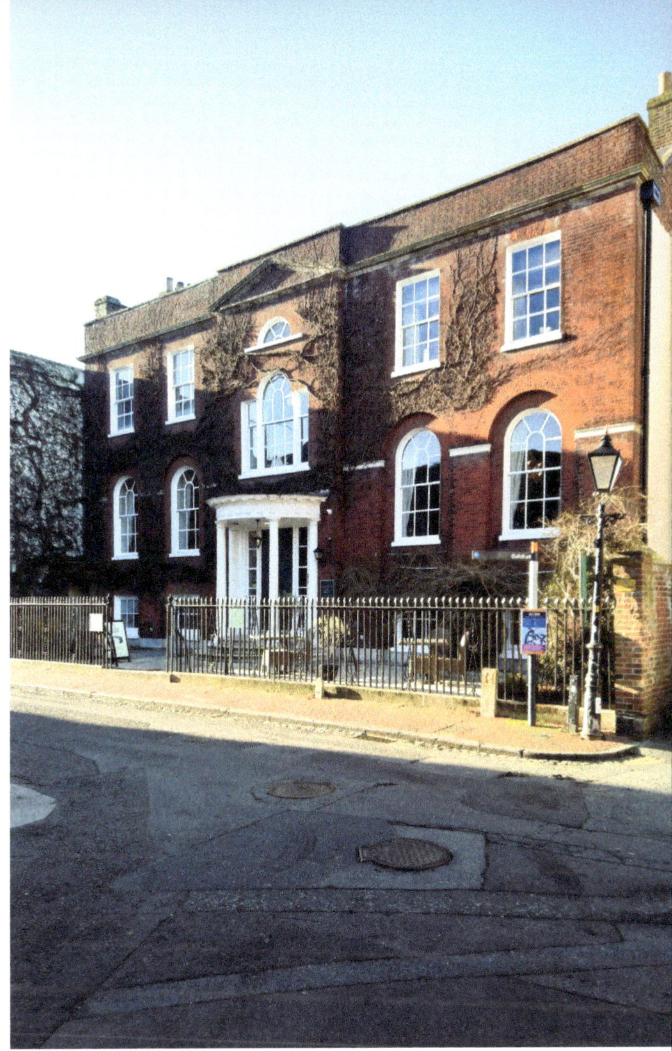

Right: Hotel du Vin.

Below: Cod fillets adorning the fireplace of what was the Lester Garland Room when the building was the Mansion House. The room is now called Port and Starboard by Hotel du Vin and is used as a conference room.

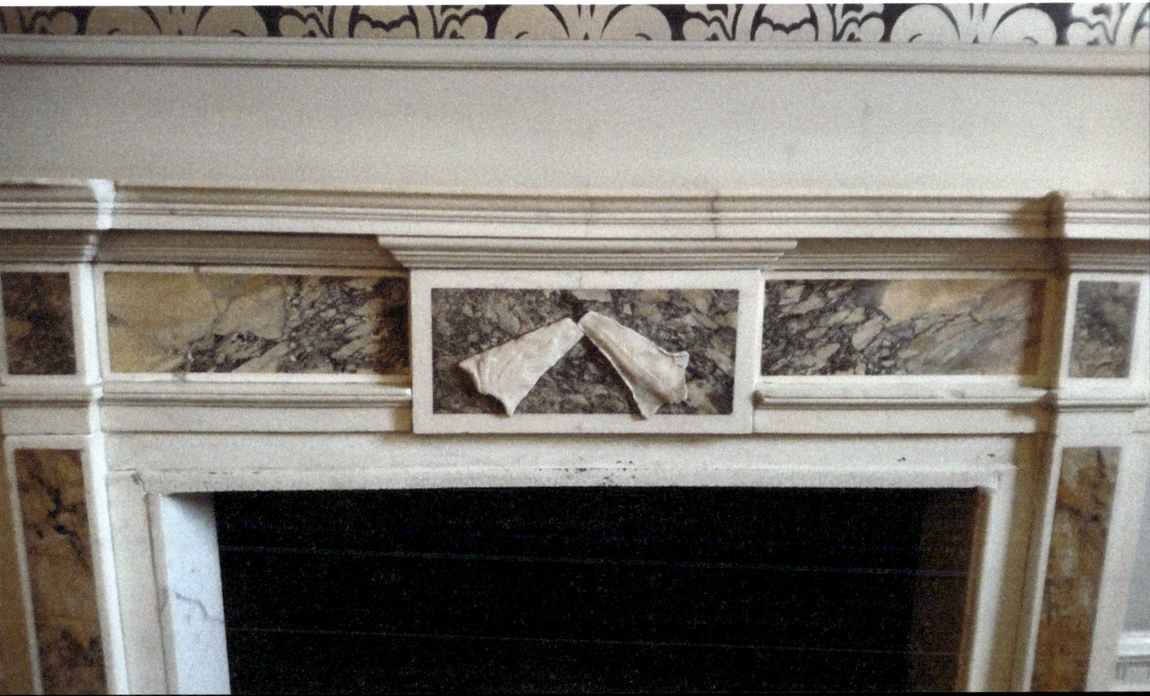

Hoys/Portsmouth Hoy

The Portsmouth Hoy pub, which is situated on the Quay, is separated from the Poole Arms by Grace House, which was once the Britannia Inn.

The Portsmouth Hoy refers to a nineteenth-century coaster which used to take people daily between Poole and Portsmouth from this section of the Quay. The hoys, as the coasters were known, were considered a more agreeable and quicker method of transport than travelling by coach and horses.

There were also hoys going to and from Swanage, Wareham, Weymouth and the Channel Islands, and the mustering point for these was further along the Quay at the King's Arms, which is now the Stable pub/restaurant.

The nautical term 'ahoy', comes from passengers hailing these types of vessels.

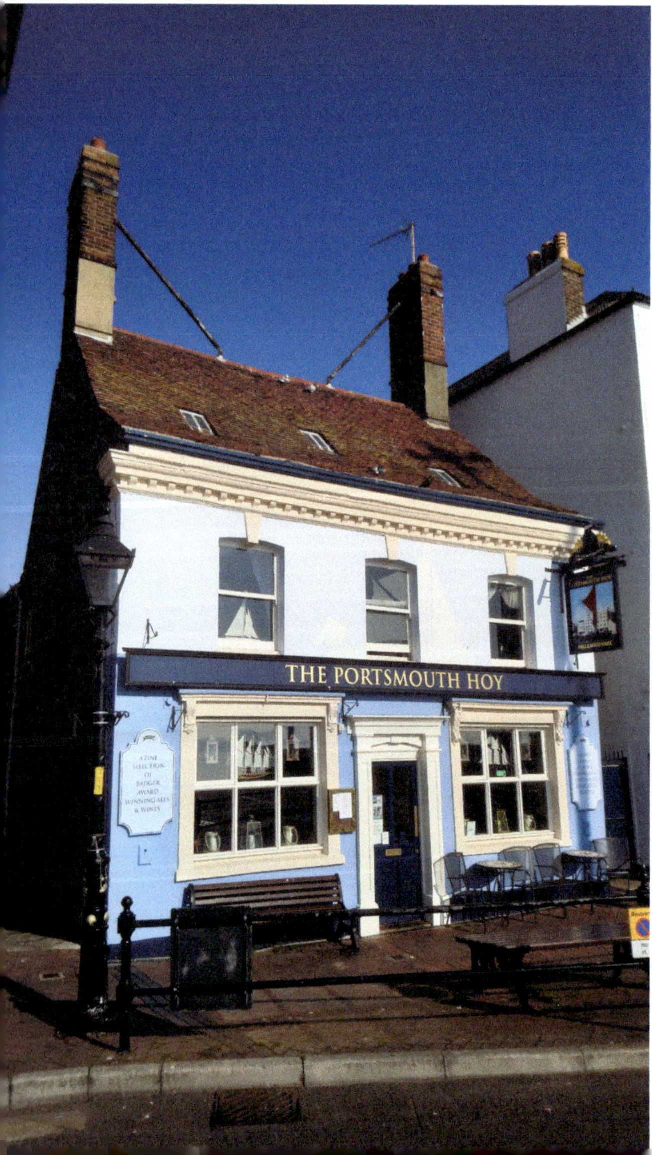

The Portsmouth Hoy.

Iron Age

The very first inhabitants of Poole were Iron Age people, as evidenced by the Iron Age log boat that was discovered in the harbour, and now resides in Poole Museum.

Channel 4's archaeological television programme *Time Team* found evidence of Iron Age commercial activity on Green Island within Poole Harbour, including the remains of an Iron Age furnace, and evidence of the production of shale jewellery. However due to the lack of shale jewellery found in the surrounding Dorset area, archaeologists have theorised that Green Island was a centre of production that exported goods to Continental Europe using log boats.

This theory lends further evidence to the belief that Green Island was an important Iron Age port. However, Tony Robinson pointed out that it seemed strange that an island within a harbour would have been a port, but apparently Green Island, Furzey Island and Brownsea Island were all one big island at that time.

Islands

There are eight islands within Poole Harbour, the largest and most famous of which is Brownsea. The others are Furzey Island (see Oil), Green Island (see Iron Age), Round Island, Long Island, Gigger's Island, Drove Island and Pergins Island in Holes Bay.

Brownsea consists of over 500 acres of woodland, open space and beaches. It is home to numerous sea birds and sika deer, and is one of the few places where Britain's native red squirrels can be sighted. It is also famous as the birthplace of scouting (see Baden-Powell), and boasts a visitor centre and an outdoor centre where such activities as archery, low ropes and den building take place. In addition, there is an outdoor theatre where visitors can enjoy the likes of Shakespeare whilst having a picnic.

Brownsea can be accessed by ferries from Poole Quay or Sandbanks, and is the only one of the eight islands that can be. However, there was a period from 1927 to 1961 when the island was owned by the reclusive Mrs Bonham-Christie, who would not allow visitors. It was during this period that Enid Blyton, whose novels are

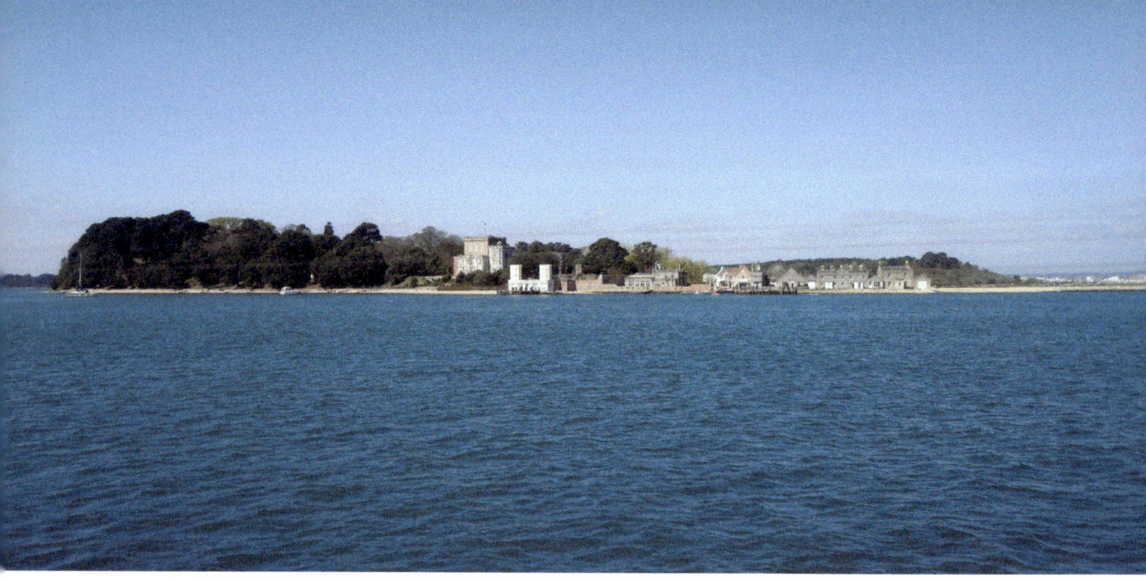

Brownsea Island.

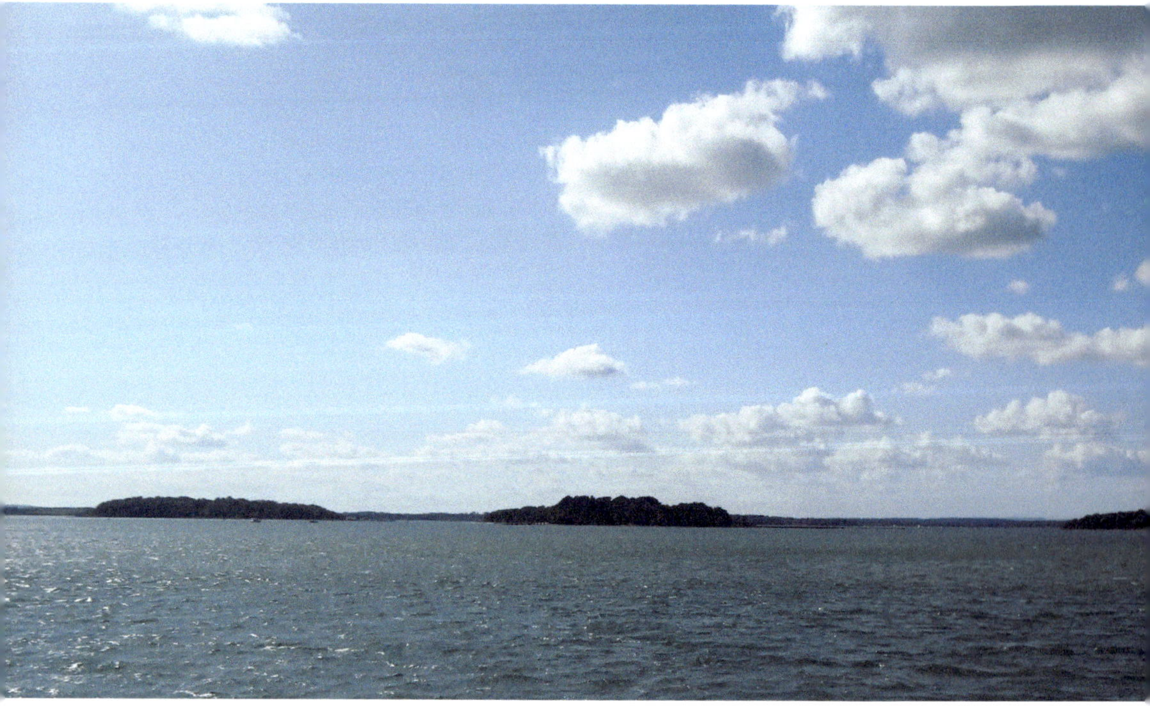

Furzey Island and Green Island.

synonymous with the Purbecks, wrote *Five Have a Mystery to Solve*, which features an island called 'Keep Away Island'.

At one time the Brownsea Ferry consisted of single muscular oarsman, Tom Wills, who rowed back and forth all day. The route he plied is still known as Will's Cut, and the markers he planted for navigational purposes are still in situ and are known as Willies.

Brownsea has been owned by the National Trust since 1962.

James – St James' Church

St James' Church was originally built in 1142, but was demolished and rebuilt in 1819. Contained within are columns constructed from Newfoundland pine, which were brought to Poole by the merchants involved in trade with Newfoundland. At the top of

Below left: St James' Church.

Below right: The Newfoundland flag flies at the top of columns constructed from Newfoundland pine.

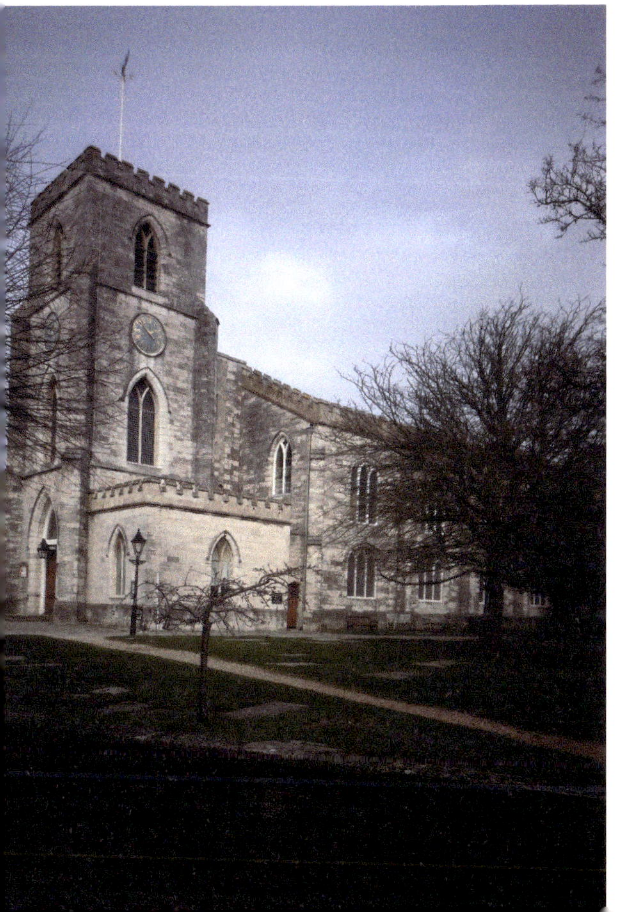

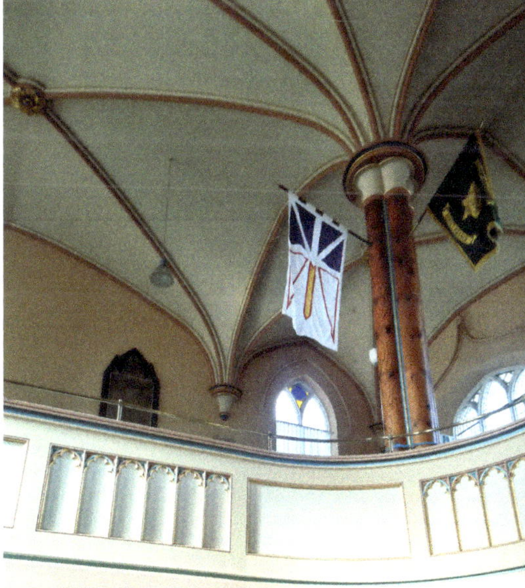

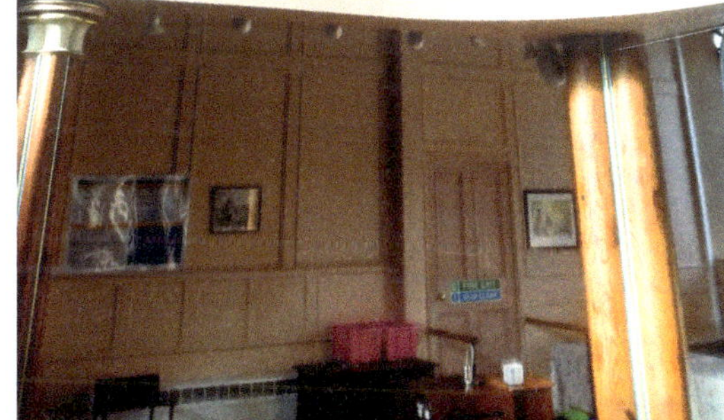

one of the columns is a Newfoundland and Labrador flag which celebrates the long-held connection between Poole and Newfoundland.

Other interesting flags that can be seen within the church include the Union Jack, which was the first British flag to fly in Paris after that city's liberation by the Allies in 1945. It was donated by Cdr Tom Sherrin, a former mayor of Poole. There is also an American flag which flew on a US coastguard cutter that took part in the D-Day landings (see D-Day Landings).

Jolliffe, Peter

This house was owned by one of the town's most prominent Newfoundland merchants, Peter Jolliffe, who purchased it in 1694 after receiving a large bounty.

The reward was given to him by King William III (William of Orange) in recognition of his bravery in going to the aid of a fishing boat which was being attacked by a

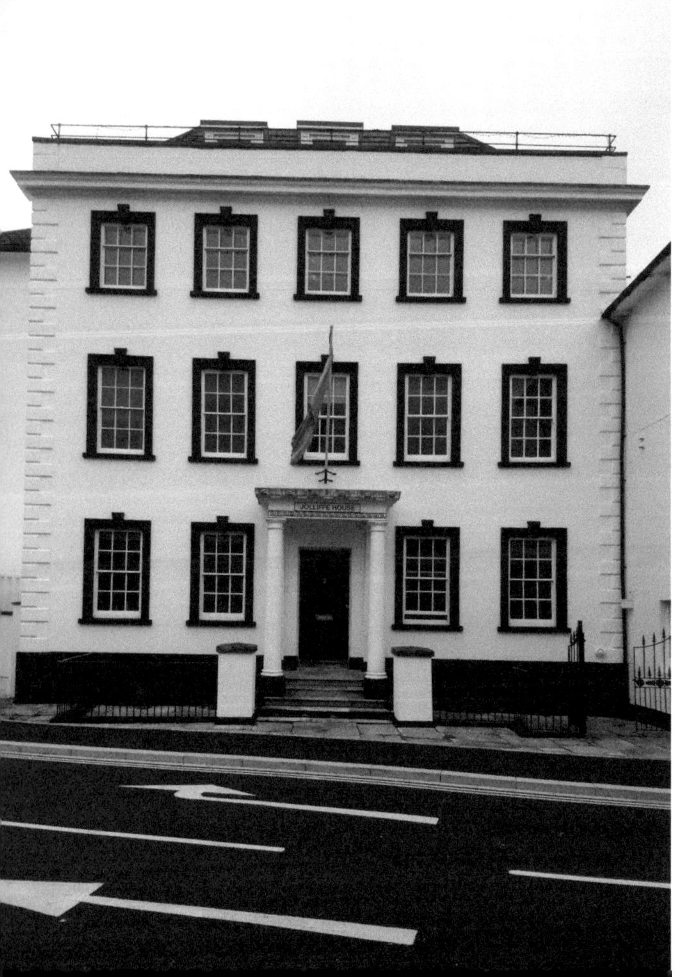

Jolliffe House.

French privateer off the coast of Weymouth. A skirmish ensued, and he eventually managed to force the privateer aground near Lulworth, where the privateer crew were taken prisoner.

His great-grandson, also Peter Jolliffe, was responsible for the rebuilding of St James' Church, and he was the rector for seventy years, from 1791 to 1861.

Rachel Allenby, a descendant of Peter Jolliffe, and a Poole developer and entrepreneur purchased the house in 1968, as well as a building on the Quay, which celebrated Poole's trade with Newfoundland in the eighteenth century, known as Newfoundland House.

Jolly Sailor

The Jolly Sailor was originally a rough and ready seamen's establishment, which had first became an alehouse in approximately 1789. It was rebuilt around 1890, and converted into the building we see on the Quay today. Like the Poole Arms (see Poole Arms), its tiled frontage came from Carters, the predecessors of Poole Pottery, and was added around 1914.

In 1908, Harry Davis became the landlord, and he frequently found himself immersed in the Quay, using his swimming and life-saving skills to save drunks who had toppled in. He was the head of the Davis dynasty that ran the Jolly Sailor for seventy years.

In the 1920s, a regular patron of the pub was a certain Thomas Edward (TE) Lawrence, or Lawrence of Arabia as he was better known.

Jolly Sailor.

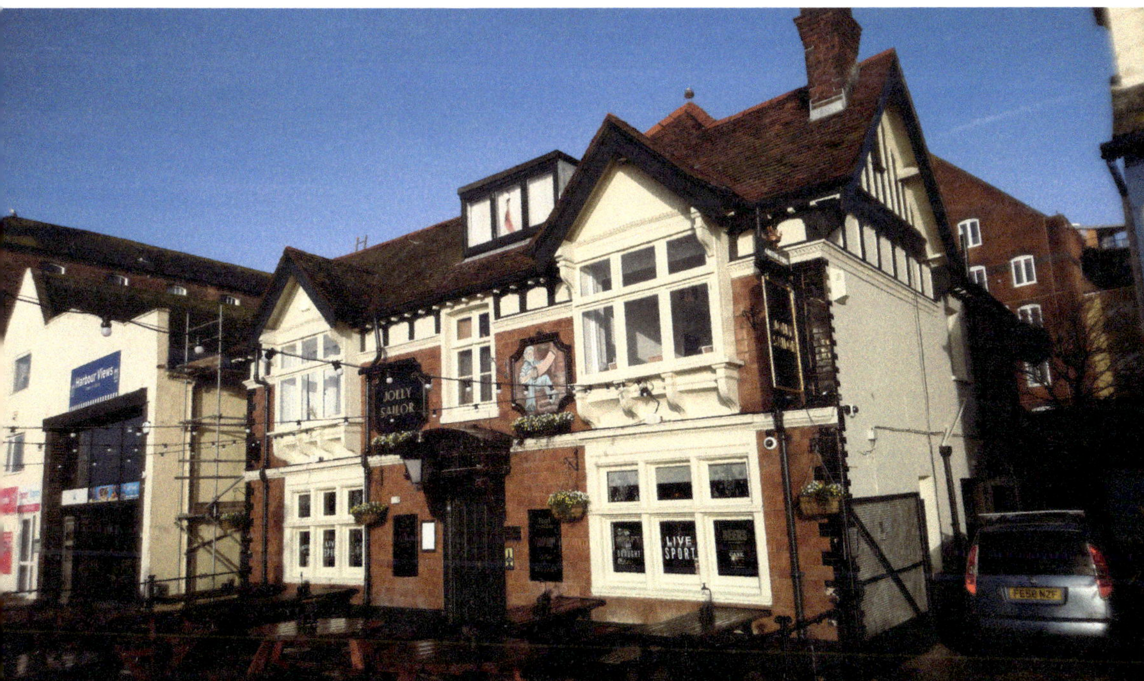

King Charles

The King Charles first became an alehouse in 1770. However, a section of the pub known as the King's Hall dates back to 1350.

The King's Hall was originally part of one large building known as the Town Cellars or Wool House (see Wool House), which became divided in the eighteenth century. It was cut through in order to provide a thoroughfare for fish and other commodities to roll through, on carts bound for markets in other Dorset towns and London. This became known as Thames Street due to its London connection, and provided an access route from the Quay to the High Street.

The main section of the pub dates back to Tudor times, including much of the brickwork and oriel panelling, whilst some of it is from the later Jacobean period. The older King's Hall section retains the original roof beams and fireplace.

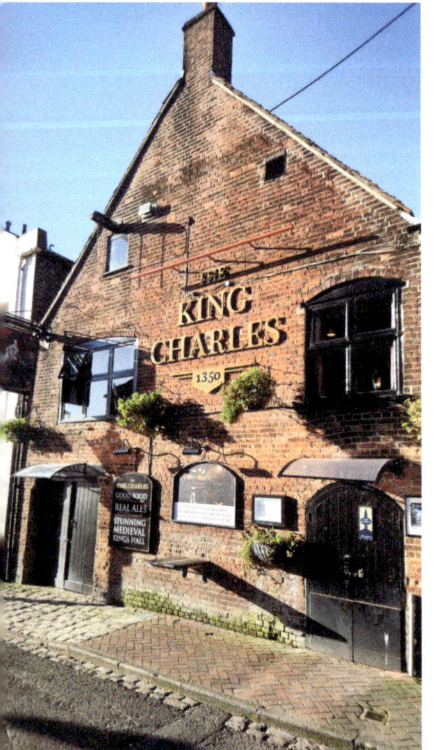

Left: The Kings Hall, part of the King Charles.

Below: The King Charles showing the Tudor part and the Kings Hall.

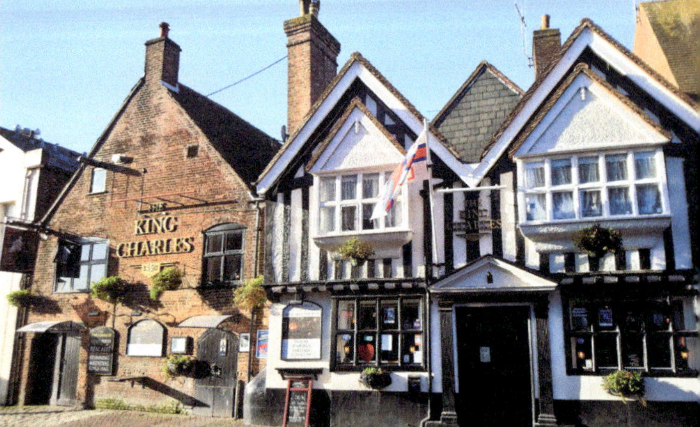

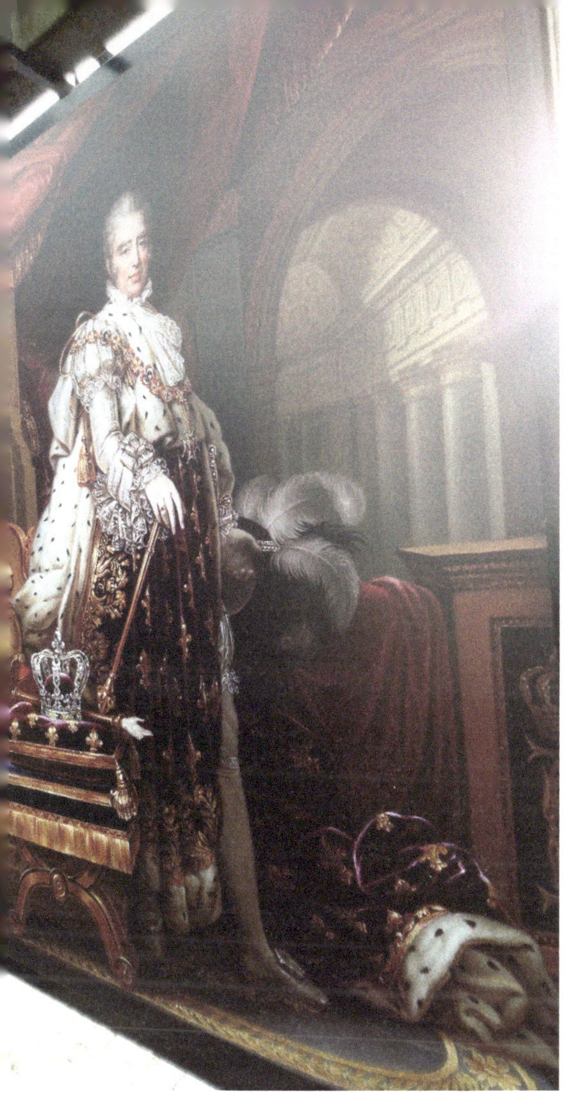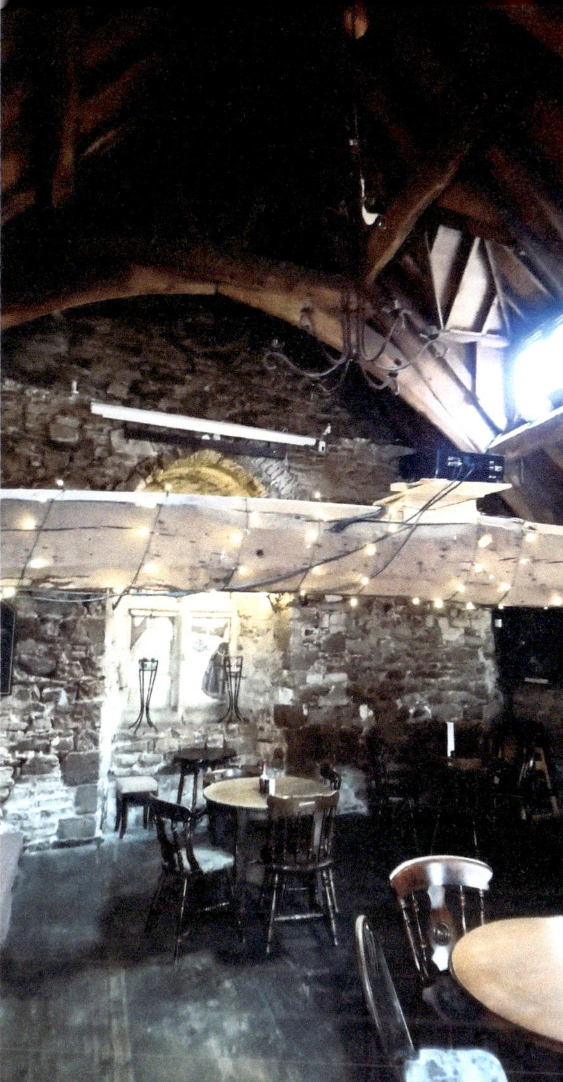

Above left: The King Charles pub sign.

Above right: Inside the Kings Hall, King Charles.

In 1830, King Charles X of France was ousted in a bloodless coup which occurred shortly after the French Revolution, and was known as the July Revolution or the Second French Revolution. He was succeeded by his cousin, who became King Louis Phillipe I.

King Charles X sought refuge in England, and landed in Poole Harbour at Hamworthy opposite Poole Quay. He was offered hospitality further along the coast at Lulworth Castle, by Dorset's principal Catholic, Joseph Weld, which he accepted. Meanwhile his family and courtiers stayed at the Antelope Hotel. They included the Duchess de Berri, the Dauphin, the Duchesse d'Angouleme and the Duke of Bordeaux, whilst the remainder of his entourage who couldn't be accommodated at the Antelope stayed at the London Tavern, which is now the Butler and Hops in Poole High Street.

The name changed to the King Charles in the early 1900s, in recognition of the exiled French king's visit to Poole.

King's Head

A pub called the Plume of Feathers, which can be traced back to 1678, was originally at the site of the King's Head, making the King's Head the second oldest pub in Poole still in operation, after the Antelope. However, some historians believe there is evidence to show that the Plume of Feathers, which may have been called the Feathers back then, pre-dates the Spanish invasion of Don Pero Nino in 1405 (see Pirates and Privateers – Harry Paye), which would then make the King's Head the oldest pub in Poole in continual usage.

The pub sign depicts Henry VIII, who is reputed to have stayed at the Plume of Feathers. He used it as a base to check the progress of a castle he was having built to defend the strategic position of the harbour entrance at Brownsea Island.

The pub was known as a notorious smuggler's haunt, and smuggler's passageways were found during restoration work. One leads to the Quay and the other to St James' Close near the church. These may well have been used by the infamous Carter gang (see Smugglers), who were known to have hidden their contraband in this pub.

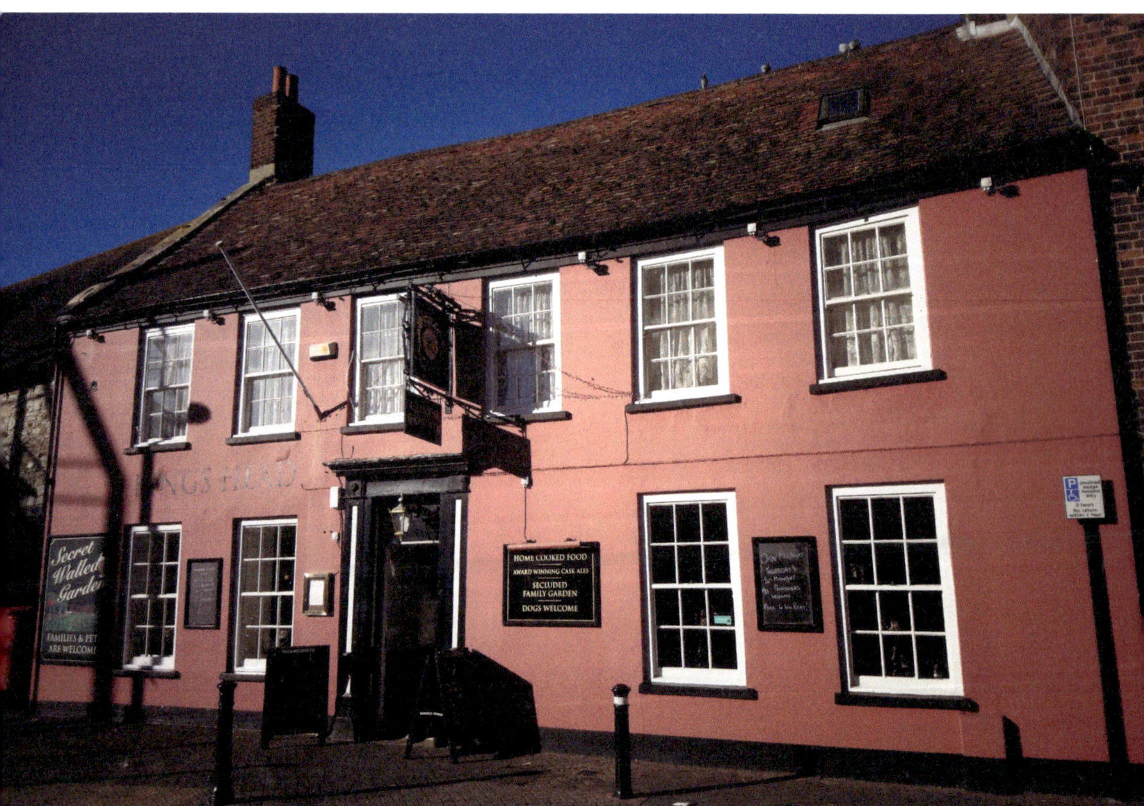

The King's Head.

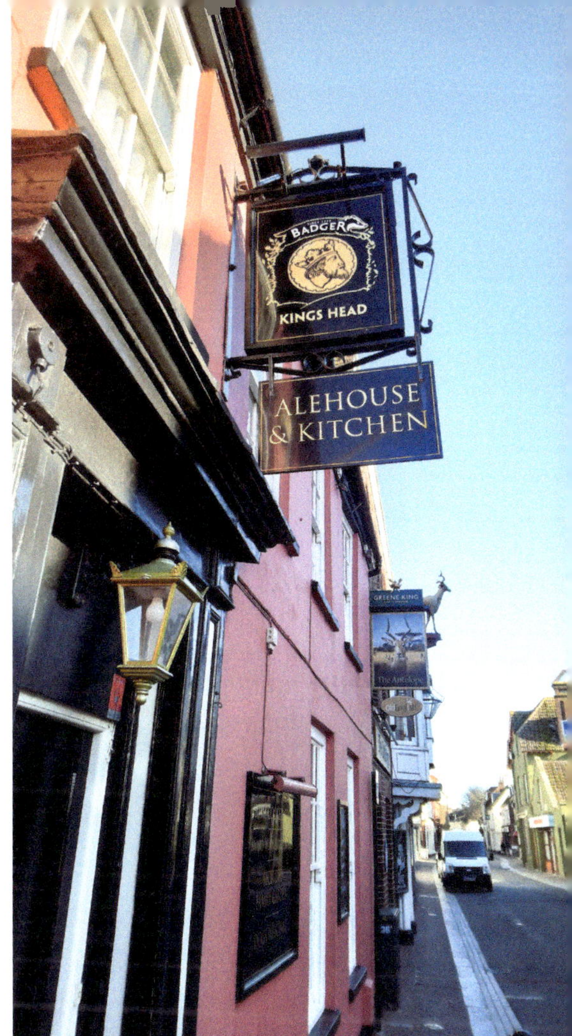

Right: The King's Head pub sign depicting Henry VIII.

Below: The castle on Brownsea Island was originally commissioned by Henry VIII to defend the strategic position of the harbour entrance, and the castle that exists on the island today still retains some of the original stonework.

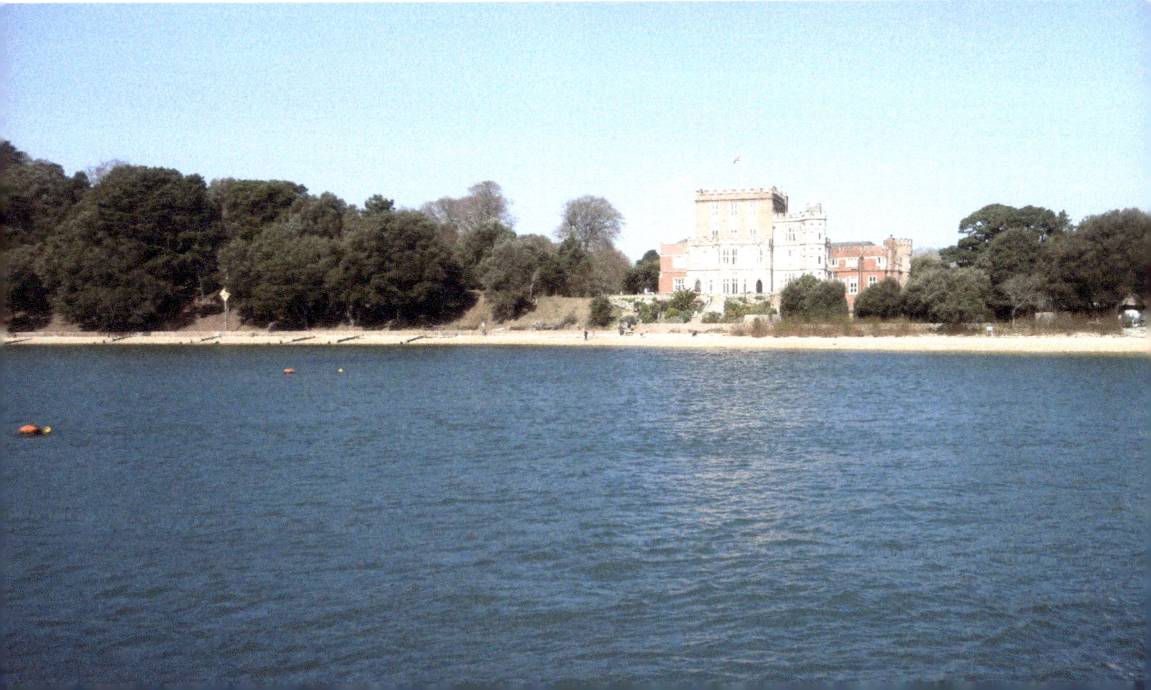

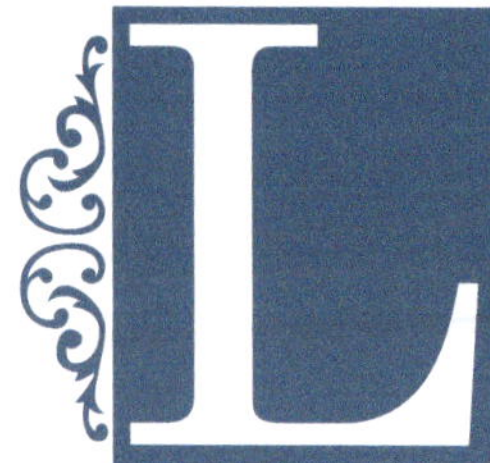

Labradors

Some of the sailors found a very useful and companionable breed of dog whilst they were in Newfoundland. They were called St John's Dogs or Lesser Newfoundlands. They were ideal for working hard in the freezing weather, retrieving fish from the cold water and helping to haul in the fishing lines. The dogs had an insatiable appetite for work and were highly cooperative.

Other experts believe that when the traders arrived in Newfoundland, there were no dogs there at all, and the dogs that subsequently became known as Labradors were the result of selective breeding of the dogs that were taken across by the Poole seamen.

The sailors often brought the dogs back on the cod ships, and they provided a popular form of transport in Poole, as passengers and equipment were pulled along in dog carts – as was the way in Newfoundland.

In the 1800s, the 2nd Earl of Malmesbury, James Harris, had heard of their qualities and became interested in them as retrievers for hunting. He found them excellent and began calling them Labradors.

At around the same time, Walter Scott, who was the 5th Duke of Buccleuch, also established kennels of St John's Dogs. The Earl of Malmesbury got to hear of this, and presented the Duke with two male St John's dogs as a gift. The Earl mated them, and by 1903, Labradors were recognised by the English Kennel Club.

There has been a growing campaign locally for Poole Council to commission a statue of a Labrador on the Quay to celebrate the town's connection with the breed, but so far this has been to no avail.

Lifting Bridge – Poole Bridge

The Lifting Bridge on the western edge of Poole Quay connects Poole to Hamworthy, and avoids a 6-mile journey around Holes Bay. It has six timetabled lifts per day, as well as some unscheduled ones, and works in synchronisation with the Twin Sails Bridge (see Twin Sails Bridge).

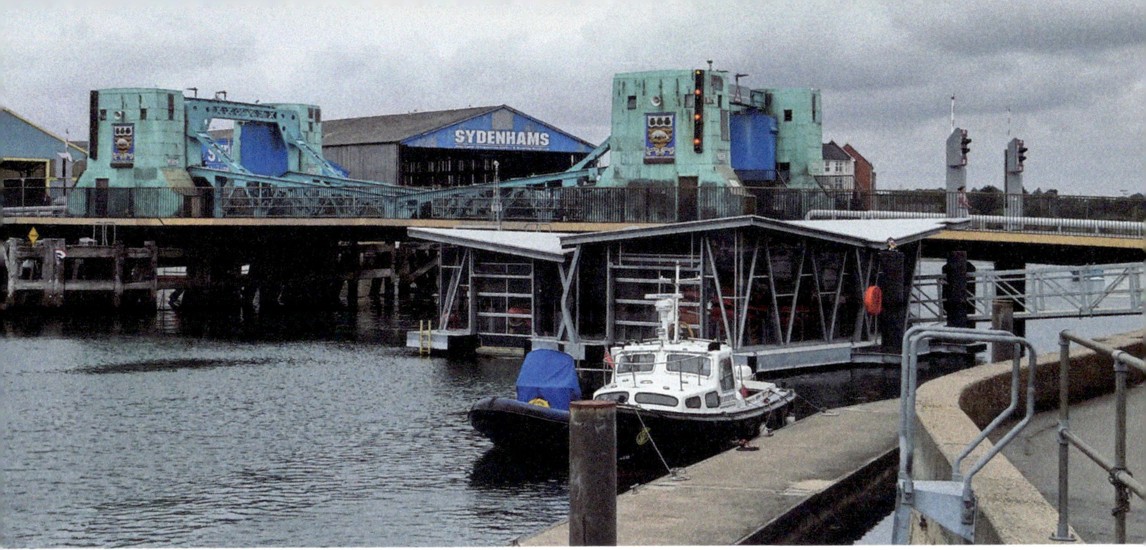

The Lifting Bridge complete with the Poole coat of arms.

The very first bridge was of a wooden construction and was initiated by William Ponsonby, the Member of Parliament for Poole, in 1834.

The current bridge is the third, and was built in 1927.

Lighthouse – Poole's Centre for the Arts

Poole Arts Centre opened in 1978, in order to provide some cultural provision for Dorset, as well as providing a new home for the renowned Bournemouth Symphony Orchestra.

It was renamed the Lighthouse in 2002, and is a centre of cultural significance nationally, as well as being a centre of excellence in the South West for live performances, film and visual art. It provides a packed programme of theatre, music, comedy, dance, film and exhibitions, and is the largest arts centre outside London.

It is the only venue in the South West to have four auditoria, which include a symphonic concert hall, a mid-scale theatre, a small-scale studio theatre and an independent cinema. There are also art galleries, function rooms, and a restaurant.

Various luminaries have performed here, and the Queen has attended twice and Princess Diana once.

The Lighthouse, Poole's centre for the arts.

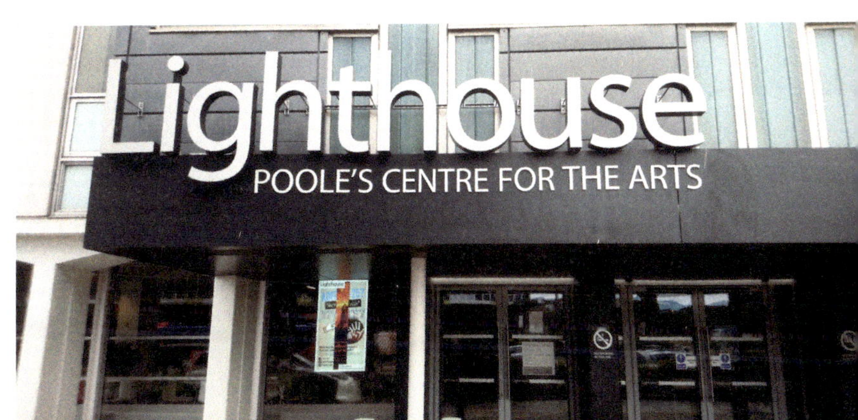

Lord Nelson

The site on the Quay, which was originally an allotment and turf house, first opened in 1764 as the Blue Boar, which was the name of the alleyway running alongside it.

In 1810, like a lot of pubs in Britain at the time, the name was changed to the Lord Nelson, in recognition of Nelson's famous victory at Trafalgar in 1805. The triumph caused great celebration but was tinged with sadness due to Nelson's death. He was held in such high regard that he was only the second commoner to be given a state funeral after Sir Isaac Newton.

It was an appropriate change of name, one might say, as many folk drinking in these quayside pubs were instrumental in Nelson's victory – although, as they supped their ale, they wouldn't have realised that they were going to be involved (see Press Gangs).

During the 1920s, the pub was frequented by the famous and flamboyant artist Augustus John during a period when he lived in Poole. There is a blue plaque on the front of the pub in acknowledgement of this (see Artists).

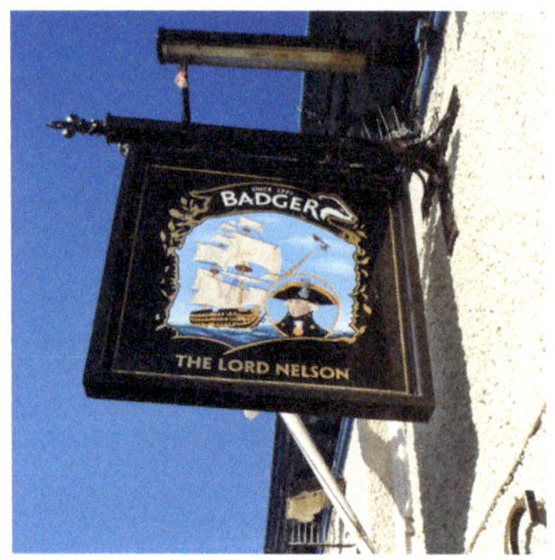

Left: The Lord Nelson pub sign.

Below: The Lord Nelson.

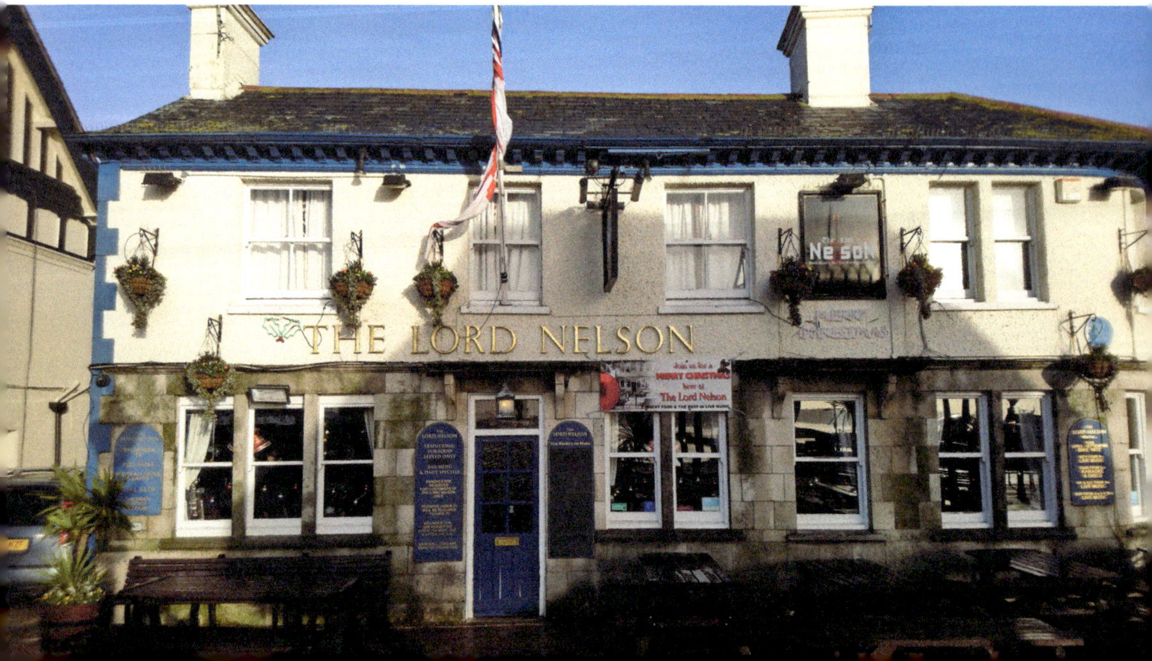

Marconi, Guglielmo

Guglielmo Marconi (1874–1937) broadcast the first ever radio signals from the Haven Hotel, Sandbanks, to the Isle of Wight in 1896, using a 120-foot mast.

Many aspects of our lives today, including radio, television, satellite links and mobile phones, owe their development to this broadcast.

The Marconi Lounge of the hotel displays photographs and information relating to the experiment, and a plaque.

Marconi chose this location because: 1. It offered an unobstructed path for the radio waves to reach the Isle of Wight; 2. Its remoteness gave him privacy from competitors; and 3. The Haven Hotel provided on-the-spot accommodation for himself, his family and his workforce.

Marconi and his family lived at the Haven Hotel between 1898 and 1926, and at this time, the Haven was one of very few buildings on the Sandbanks peninsular.

Haven Hotel.

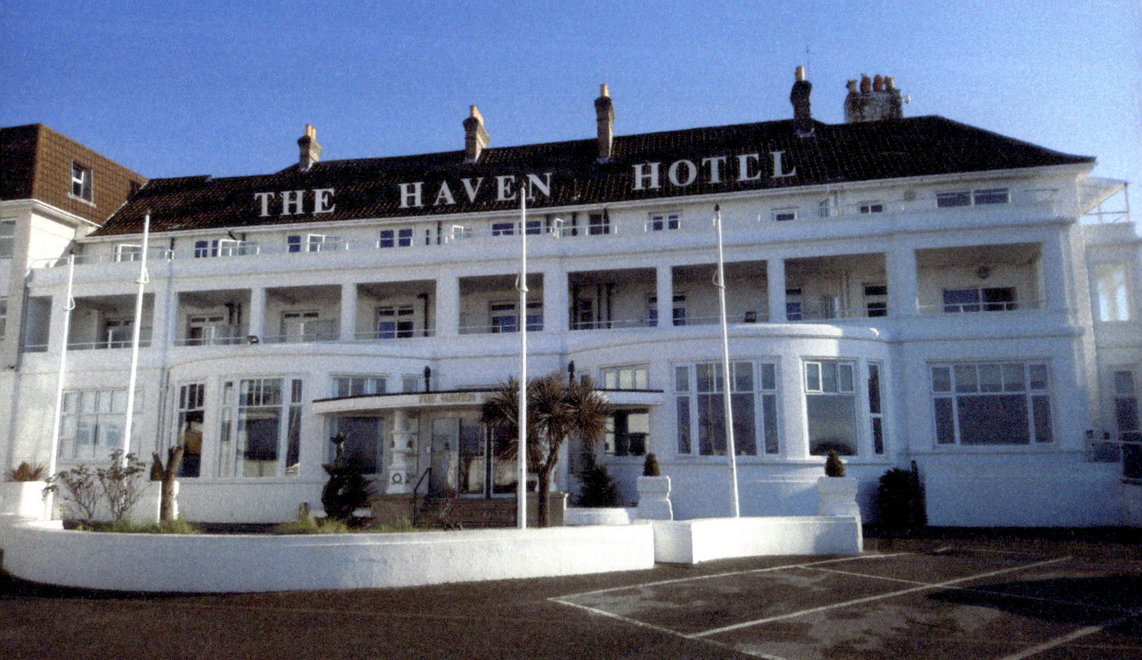

The success of this experiment allowed him to subsequently transmit the first transatlantic radio message from Angrouse Cliffs, just south of Poldhu cove near Mullion in Cornwall, in which three dots (S in Morse code) were received in Newfoundland on 12 December 1901.

Monmouth – Duke of

Poole was a great stronghold for the Parliamentarians in the English Civil War (1642–51). Nevertheless, following the restoration of the monarchy, King Charles II and his illegitimate son, the Duke of Monmouth (1649–85), were greeted with great enthusiasm in the town when they paid a visit in 1665.

They were entertained to a banquet at the house of Colonel William Skutt, who was keen to extend an olive branch, despite the fact that he had been a staunch Parliamentarian, and had been involved in a siege which resulted in the Parliamentarians gaining control of nearby Corfe Castle.

There is a plaque on the building where the banquet took place (now a Sainsbury's), and the wording refers to the 'unfortunate' Monmouth, which is a reference to the failed Monmouth Rebellion of 1685 against the Catholic James II (King Charles II's brother and Monmouth's uncle).

The rebellion started at Lyme Regis and ended in a massacre at the Battle of Sedgemoor, after which Monmouth, along with three comrades, fled across the Somerset border into Dorset in an attempt to get to Poole and flee the country. He got within a whisker of Poole, but was captured on Horton Heath, whereupon he was taken to be identified by the nearest magistrate, who was Anthony Ettrick of Holt Lodge, the recorder of the Borough of Poole. Ettrick ordered him to be taken to the Tower of London, where he faced execution at the hands of an unskilled executioner, Jack Ketch, on Tower Hill.

The first blow of Ketch's axe bounced off leaving only a slight wound, and then several more strikes were required before poor Monmouth died, and even then his head had to be cut from his body with a knife.

This was only the beginning of the reprisals, as Dorset and other western counties suffered severe consequences for the failed rebellion, as the feared and loathed Judge Jeffreys wrought shocking and violent retribution in the form of the Bloody Assizes.

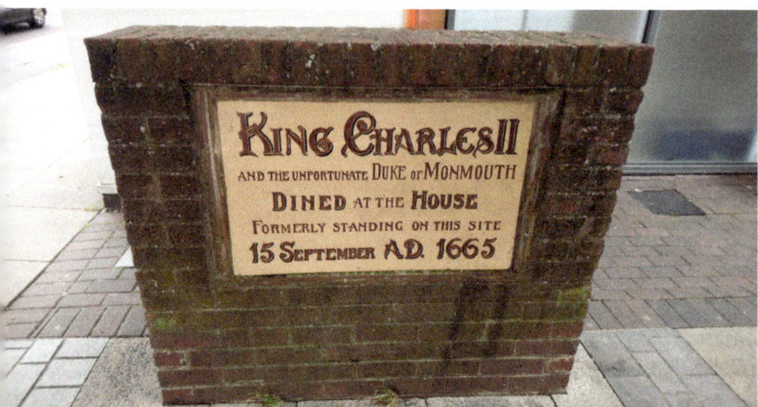

Monmouth plaque.

Poole hosted many of the executions (see Execution Site), as the ill-fated rebels who had been sentenced to be hanged, drawn and quartered were farmed out to various locations in Dorset after having been convicted of High Treason at Dorchester.

Motorcycle Speedway

Motorcycle speedway racing has taken place at Poole Stadium every year since 1948, and Poole Pirates are one of the best-supported and most successful sides in the world.

They provide a wonderful spectacle and display breathtaking skill as they accelerate along the straights and skid round the corners, roared on by the fanatical home support.

The Poole Pirates have routinely won major honours throughout their history, and the stadium has hosted test and representative matches against Poland, Sweden, America, New Zealand, the Soviet Union and Australia. Indeed, the Pirates were the first British club side to undertake an overseas tour, when they visited Sweden in 1948.

In 2004, temporary stands had to be erected to host a record crowd of over 7,000, when Poole Stadium hosted the Speedway World Cup, in which Sweden defeated Great Britain in the final.

However, the story of the Poole Pirates has not always been one of unbridled success, as in 1985 they went into liquidation. However, they survived by combining with Dorset neighbours Weymouth Wildcats, who were also struggling at that time, as their ground had been sold for redevelopment. They formed a team called Poole Wildcats, but two years later, reverted to Poole Pirates and the rest is history.

Poole Pirates motorcycle speedway.

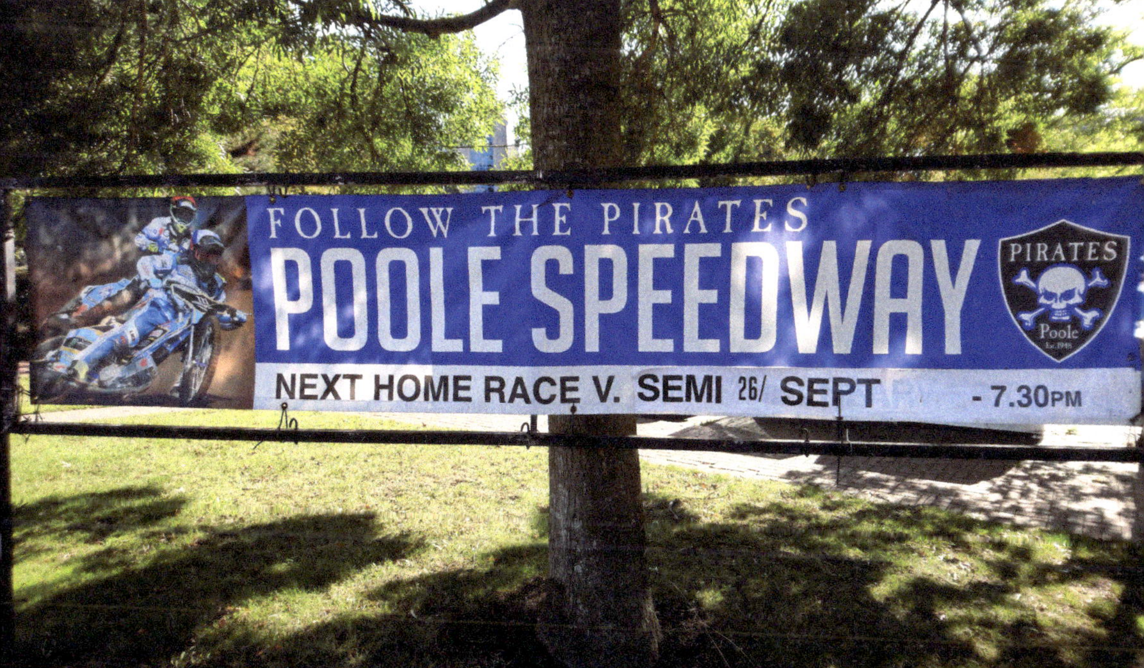

Newfoundland Trade

In 1497, John Cabot, the Italian navigator and explorer, sailed west from Bristol on the commission of King Henry VII, with the objective of finding a passage to Asia, just as Christopher Columbus had tried previously. Unfortunately, Cabot also failed to achieve his actual objective; but like Columbus, he did discover a northern part of the American Continent, which, with great originality, he called Newfoundland.

He noted that the seas in this vicinity were so full of cod that they were actually preventing the ship from making headway. Word of this spread throughout the West Country, and was paid particular heed to in Poole.

This heralded a golden age for Poole, as merchants seized the opportunity, and became pre-eminent in the business of catching cod, and then exchanging the cod for other commodities.

Newfoundland Trade depicted pictorially in the tiles of a housing development at Barbers Wharf.

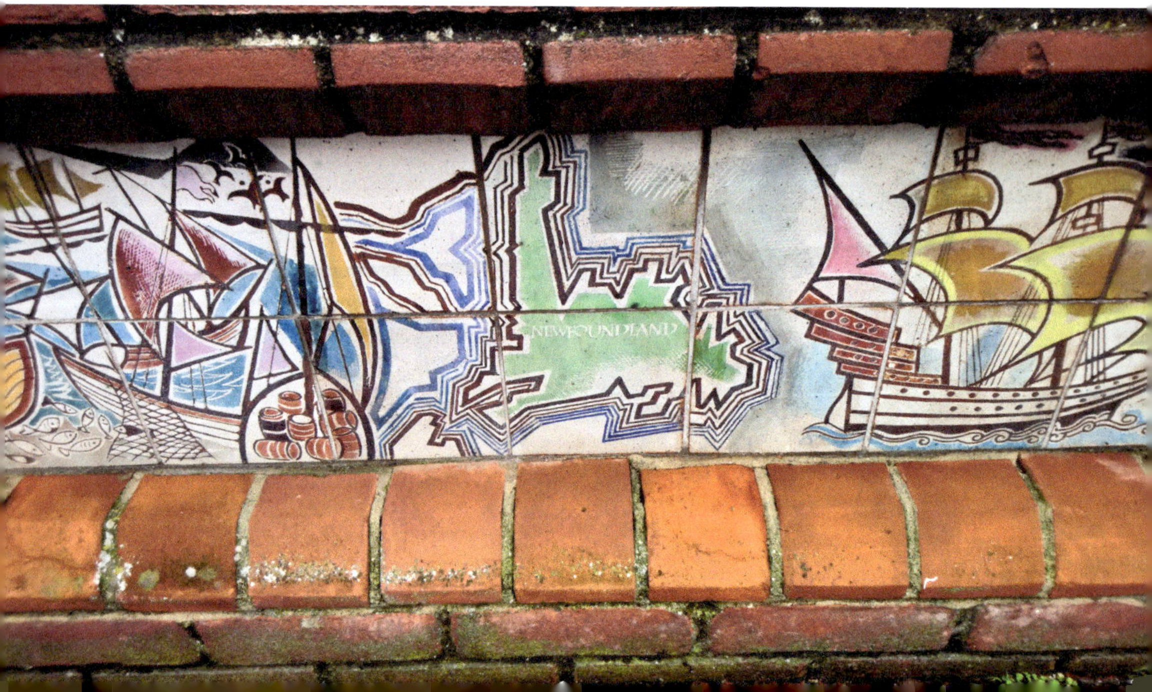

Every spring, hundreds of merchants from Poole sailed across the Atlantic to the cod-rich Grand Banks of Newfoundland. They also took with them goods and commodities that could be exchanged for furs, seal skins and cranberries.

They took much of the cod to Mediterranean countries and the West Indies. In the Mediterranean they traded cod for almonds, figs, olive oil, salt, lemons and wine; whereas in the West Indies the cod was used to feed the slaves on the sugar plantations, and traded for molasses and rum. They returned to Poole in the autumn with these goods, along with the cod, furs, seal skins and cranberries.

The Newfoundland trade really started to take off in the seventeenth century, but was at its absolute zenith in the late eighteenth century. At this time, thousands of people from Poole and Newfoundland were employed in the triangular trade – as it became known – and by 1790, 230 ships and 1,500 seamen were sailing to Newfoundland every spring.

The merchants grew rich, and as a spin-off, Poole as a town also became wealthy, as local businesses and tradesmen really began to focus on the trade.

Many Poole fishermen stayed in Newfoundland for the winter, which in turn further generated the economy of Poole, as the food, clothing, fishing equipment, ropes, sails and leather were all being produced in Poole.

In the nineteenth century, the Napoleonic Wars, which began in 1803, boosted trade, as Britain and Spain were allied against the French and had a trade agreement. There was also a blockade of the Danish fishing fleet, meaning that British vessels had a monopoly on the sale of cod to Spain.

Trade increased further when Wellington was victorious in the Peninsular War, opening up the markets of Portugal and Italy.

The Poole merchants even managed to trade with France, despite Britain being at war with them. They achieved this by using a similar triangular trading system involving Poole, the Channel Islands and France. The Channel Islands were still trading with France, whereas British vessels were not allowed to.

The Poole merchants supplied grain, cloth and horses to the Channel Islands and returned to Poole with goods originally from France, such as wine, cream and salt.

The wealth of the Newfoundland merchants brought them power, and they wielded a lot of influence in Poole, taking up positions of eminence such as mayor, or as Members of Parliament. They also had huge influence with the government in Newfoundland.

However, after the Battle of Waterloo in 1815, and hence the end of the Napoleonic Wars, the bottom dropped out of the salted cod market, and the Newfoundland trade ceased as many traders went bankrupt.

During the Napoleonic Wars there had been a great demand for fish in Mediterranean countries, as there was a shortage of other commodities. However, in peacetime, these commodities were freely available, meaning there was less demand for fish. Also, their own fishing fleets could now safely put to sea. Plus, fleets from America also started to get in on the action, increasing competition in what was a shrinking market, with the price of cod falling.

There was a brief renaissance of the trade in the early 1820s, but by 1828, only ten British ships were still plying the old triangular route and by 1860, the Newfoundland trade had ceased altogether.

Many sailors from Poole elected to stay in Newfoundland rather than return to an uncertain future. Many stayed simply because they couldn't afford the fare for the passage home. Those that stayed in Newfoundland switched to the seal fur trade or the timber trade. Others returned to Poole and turned their hand to oyster fishing or transporting coal.

The legacy of the wealth generated by the Newfoundland trade can still be seen in the fine, well-preserved Georgian mansions around St James' Church, Market Street and Thames Street, in the heart of the Old Town, where a conservation area has been established to preserve these buildings for posterity.

It is said that today, a third of Newfoundlanders can trace their ancestry back to Poole, and the heritage of the Newfoundland trade lives on in many Poole street names, for instance Cabot Lane, Garland Road, Jolliffe Road, Newfoundland Drive and Labrador Drive. Poole's cultural links with Newfoundland have been re-cemented in recent years with societies from both sides of the pond making exchange visits.

Oil

In 1959, oil was discovered in Dorset at Kimmeridge Bay in the Purbecks. Later, during the energy crisis of the 1970s, further exploration for Dorset oil took place, which led to the discovery of huge reserves, extending for several miles underneath Poole Harbour and Poole Bay.

Furzey Island, which lies to the south-west of Brownsea and after Brownsea is the second largest island in Poole Harbour, was earmarked as the best place to access the oil, and it now forms part of the Wytch Farm Oilfield.

Production started in 1979, and the site has been developed by BP into the most productive onshore oil well in mainland Britain, although nowadays, the Anglo-French firm Perenco owns the majority stake.

Most people living in Poole would be unaware of the vast industrial production taking place on the island, and in fact the sensitive manner in which production has

Furzey Island.

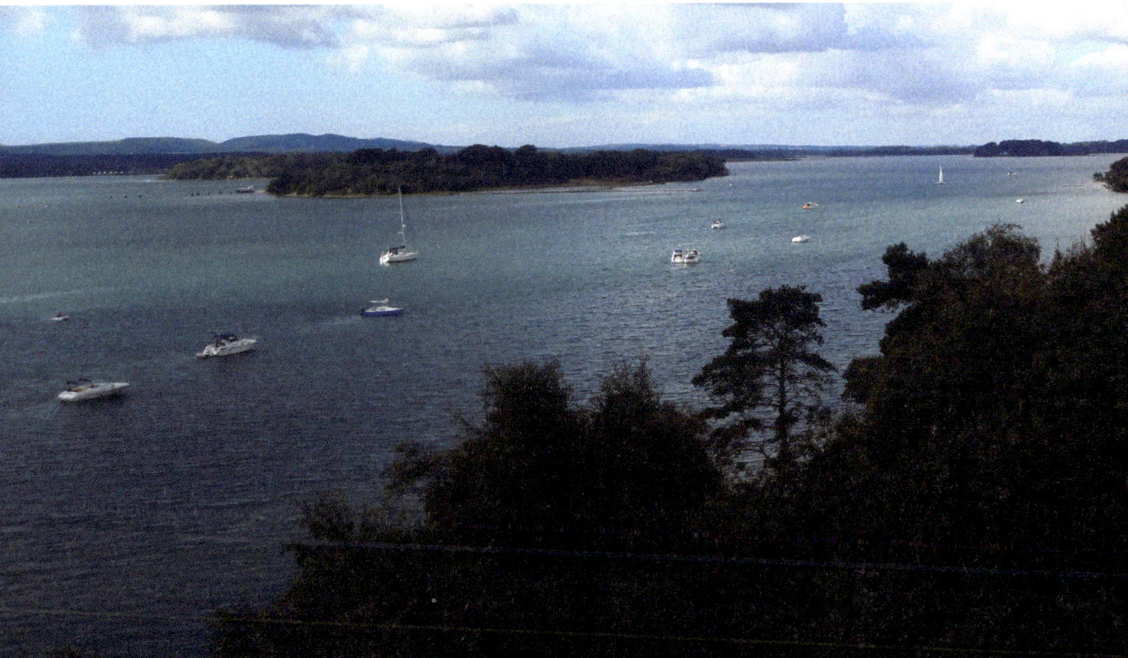

been carried out led to BP being the recipient of the Queen's Award for Environmental Achievement in 1995.

The measures which have been taken include buildings situated on sites which have been excavated to reduce their height, and the painting of buildings in a dull brown colour to help them blend in. Also, the oil wells only occupy 5 acres of the available 31. However, hidden in the trees are twenty-two oil wells split into two sites, from which the oil is pumped through pipes for processing at Wytch Farm processing plant, near Wareham, and then to Hamble on Southampton water for further processing.

In 2019, another energy firm, Orallion, showed an interest in the oil reserves around Poole, and have carried out some exploratory drilling in Poole Bay. They have established that there is potential to extract fifteen million barrels of oil from the area. Quite what impact that would have on the area's beaches is a moot point.

Pirates and Privateers

The Newfoundland merchants probably earned their vast wealth, as sailing to and from Newfoundland would have certainly been no picnic.

They had to contend with the French Navy at a time of hostilities with France, but a greater problem in the earlier days of Newfoundland trading was having to run the gauntlet of French and Spanish pirates, as well as those from North Africa. However, Poole was hardly whiter than white in this respect, as the town certainly had its fair share of home-grown pirates, who also ambushed the Newfoundland traders.

The Newfoundland merchants appealed to the Crown to offer protection, but their appeals fell on deaf ears. This is one reason why Poole supported the Parliamentarians during the English Civil War.

A Privateer was the owner of a private warship that was authorised by the government to attack ships from countries that England was at war with. They were also authorised to take them as prizes, and sell off the ship and the cargo, a percentage of which went to the Crown.

Privateers were an accepted part of naval warfare in the seventeenth, eighteenth and nineteenth centuries, as it was a way of mobilising ships to cause maximum disruption to the enemy. However, the boundaries between privateers and piracy were often blurred, as the reality was that privateers were often pirates who took advantage of wars to carry out legalised piracy.

Between 1626 and 1629, at least twelve Poole-based pirates were given 'letters of marque' permitting them to become privateers, specifically to encourage them to attack French and Spanish ships at the time of the Anglo-French War.

By the end of the nineteenth century, the practice of privateering had fallen out of favour due to the chaos it caused, and because it encouraged piracy.

Notorious Poole Pirates

John Broom

Poole-based privateer/pirate who on one occasion brought in a vessel bound from Nantes to Dunkirk, laden with brandy, silk, coffee and other goods.

Thomas Canaway

In 1408, Thomas Canaway was among the pirates suspected of capturing a large number of ships from Brittany, and a warrant was issued for his arrest, despite him being the mayor of Poole at the time. He was known to be an associate of Poole's most notorious pirate, Harry Paye.

Stephen Heynes

In 1583, the Admiralty sent armed ships to purge the pirates of Studland Bay. They rounded up nine pirate captains who were subsequently hanged, but Stephen Heynes managed to avoid capture. He once captured a ship from Dieppe named the *Endurance*, and brought it into Studland. Its cargo included parrots and macaws, which of course made him very popular with his fellow pirates. He also captured vessels from Scotland and Plymouth.

Harry Paye

Harry Paye was Poole's most notorious and prolific pirate, and is so indelibly associated with Poole that he even has a geographical feature named after him, 'Old Harry' – a chalk stack standing in the sea at Handfast Point on the Isle of Purbeck. The stack marks the Jurassic Coast's most easterly point.

He was reputedly born around 1360, on the corner of Hill Street and Carters Lane, where there is now an electricity substation.

He terrorised the Spanish and French coastline in the late fourteenth and early fifteenth centuries, acting in typical pirate fashion, setting towns ablaze, stealing ships and taking hostages for ransom. He gained wealth and infamy, as well as the discreet endorsement of King Henry IV, as England was at war with France at this time.

Old Harry.

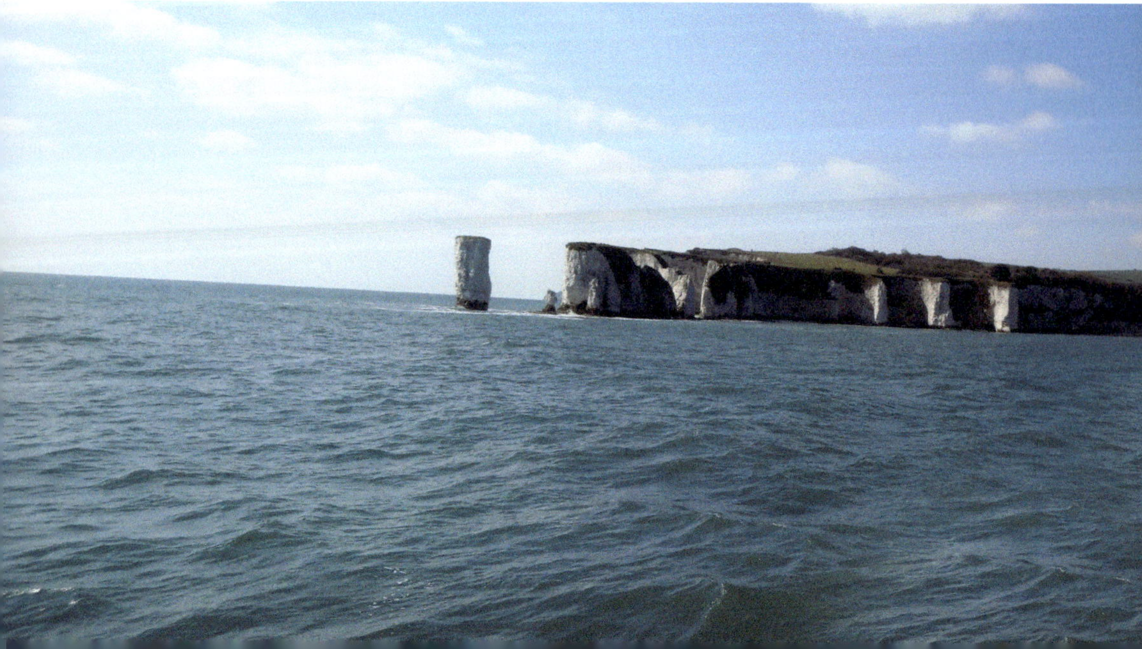

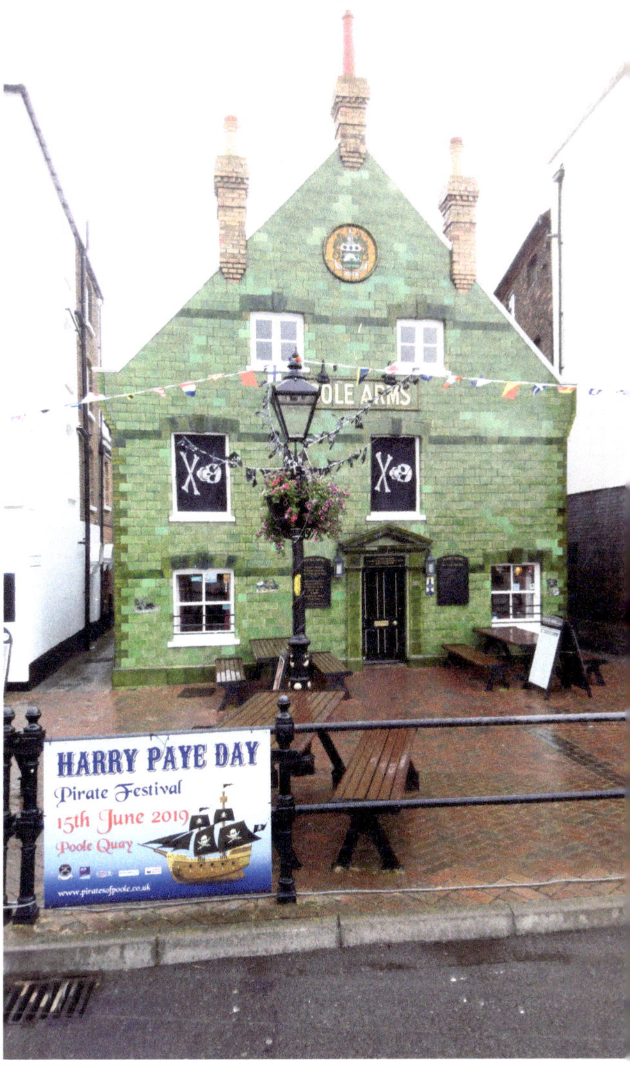

The Poole Arms decked out for the
Harry Paye Fun Day.

Ironically the reason he was so often on the Spanish coast was that he was transporting pilgrims to Galicia in Northern Spain (see Coat of Arms) in his other role as a sea captain. However, when he arrived in Spain, worship was usually the last thing on his mind, and it would be hard to find a more unlikely pilgrim, as he set about ransacking the place.

On one occasion, he so incensed the Spanish by stealing a valuable and very holy gold crucifix from the Church of Santa Maria in Finisterra, that in 1405, the Spanish, under the command of Don Pero Nino, invaded Poole in a revenge attack. They set the area around the Great Quay on fire, but were unable to find *Arripay*, as they called him, as he was away at sea. However, they did succeed in killing his brother in a pitched battle.

After having initially been taken by surprise in the dawn raid, Poole's seasoned longbowmen started to get their act together and began to find their range, exacting a heavy toll of dead and wounded from the Spanish as they were driven back to their ships. Archery was frequently practised in England at this time, between the battles of Crecy and Agincourt, and in fact, football was banned for a period to ensure that people did practice.

On another occasion in 1407, Harry sailed into town with 120 captured vessels laden with iron, salt, oil and wine. Apparently, the people of Poole declared the occasion an unofficial public holiday as they proceeded to tuck into the wine.

Sometime after 1407, Harry left his native Poole and moved to Kent where he married and had a son. He died in 1419 and is buried at Faversham in Kent.

Poole still celebrates his dubious legacy with a Harry Paye Fun Day every June, usually around the fifteenth. It involves, among other things, a parade of pirates along the Quay and various performances of sea shanties, whilst raising money for local charities.

John Piers

John Piers was actually a notorious Cornish pirate who was based in Padstow. However, he marauded around the coastline from the Bristol Channel to the Isle of Wight.

In 1581, his mother was accused of being a witch, and in the same year, Piers was caught bringing a large haul ashore at Studland Bay. He was arrested, but bribed the jailer of Dorchester jail to escape, before being recaptured and subsequently hanged in 1582.

Meanwhile his mother was acquitted of her own conviction, and is said to have hidden her son's remaining loot in the cliffs at Harlyn Bay, Cornwall.

Pirates of Studland Bay

Pirates in Studland Bay preyed upon shipping using Poole Harbour, and many of the innkeepers were in league with them. The merchants of Poole implored the government to help, and eventually there was a purge in 1583, which resulted in numerous hangings. However, to the dismay of the Newfoundland traders, these setbacks didn't stop the pirates continuing to plunder their ships.

Poole Arms

The Poole Arms is a Grade II listed building which dates from 1572, making it the oldest pub situated on the Quay.

In 1850, it suffered a serious fire, which resulted in the destruction of the flour company next door.

The building is very distinctive, as it is adorned with green tiles. These were added shortly after the fire, and were supplied by Carter's Tiles of Hamworthy, who were the predecessors of the world-renowned Poole Pottery.

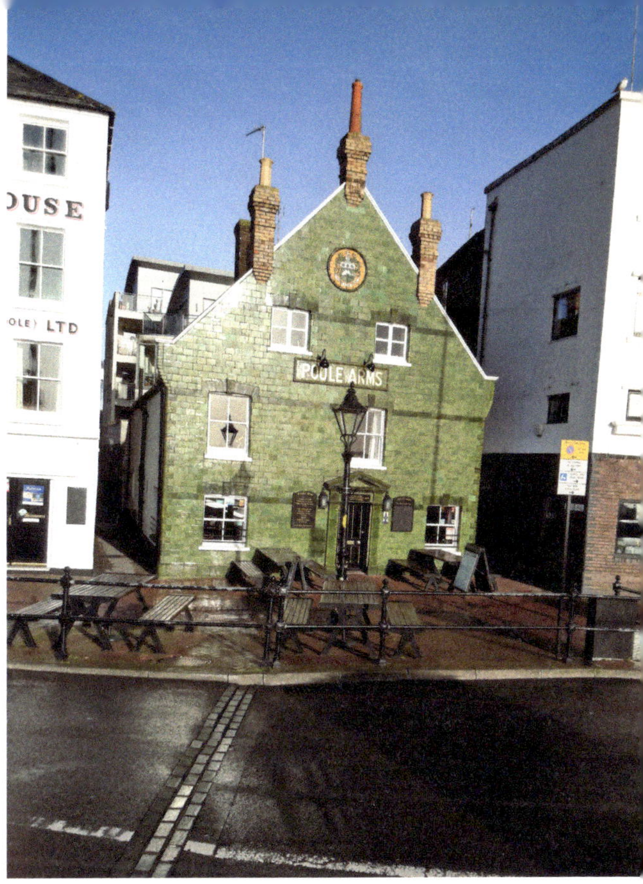

The Poole Arms as it normally looks.

High up on the front of the building is a disc of tiles making up the Poole coat of arms, with the town motto underneath (see Coat of Arms).

This, like many Poole pubs, is reputed to have more spirits than those dispensed by the optics.

Pottery

Poole has been a centre for pottery manufacture for centuries, as it has easy access to clay and limestone from the Purbeck Hills.

Poole Pottery was originally 'Carters Industrial Tile Manufactory', which was founded in 1873 after Jesse Carter took over a struggling ornamental brick and tile company called Walker's Pottery. In 1895, he was able to expand, and also bought out another firm called Architectural Pottery. The business flourished to such a degree that many of the tiles on the London Underground were made by Carter's.

In the 1920s, Jesse Carter combined with potters John and Trudy Adams and designers Harold and Phoebe Stabler to become Poole Pottery. They made world-famous pottery from a factory on Poole Quay at the original site founded by Jesse Carter.

They moved from the Quay to another site in Poole in 2001, and then eventually closed in 2006. However, a presence on the Quay is still maintained, in the form of a retail

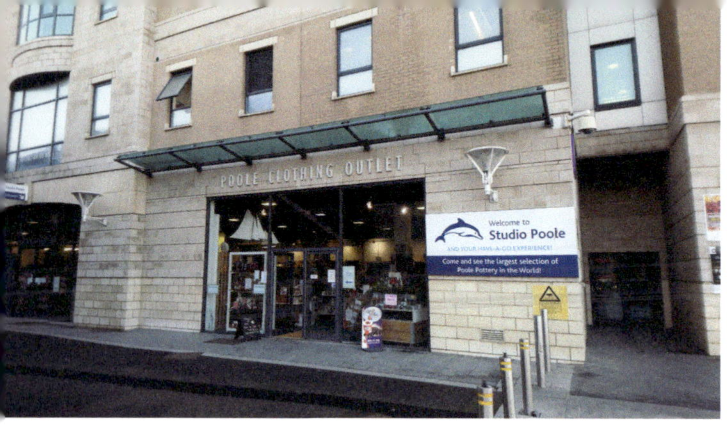

Poole Pottery still maintains a presence on the Quay.

outlet at the old premises, which houses the largest selection of Poole Pottery in the world and hosts demonstrations of pottery making for visitors. The rest of the former site is a block of 105 luxury apartments, shops and restaurants called Dolphin Quays.

The name of Poole Pottery still lives on with collectable items still being sold in the likes of Harrods or Tiffany & Co. of New York. However, the pottery is now made in Stoke-on-Trent as part of Stafford Tableware Ltd.

The Carter family became eminent locally, and have been responsible for the establishment of schools in the area; for instance, Herbert Carter School, now called Carter Community School, in Hamworthy.

Powder House

In 1775, a powder house was built in the vicinity of the old windmill in Windmill Field. The purpose of the building was to protect Poole Quay from explosions, by requiring mariners carrying gunpowder to deposit it here, before entering the harbour. Also, during the Napoleonic Wars the gunpowder was stored here, before being loaded onto ships of the line.

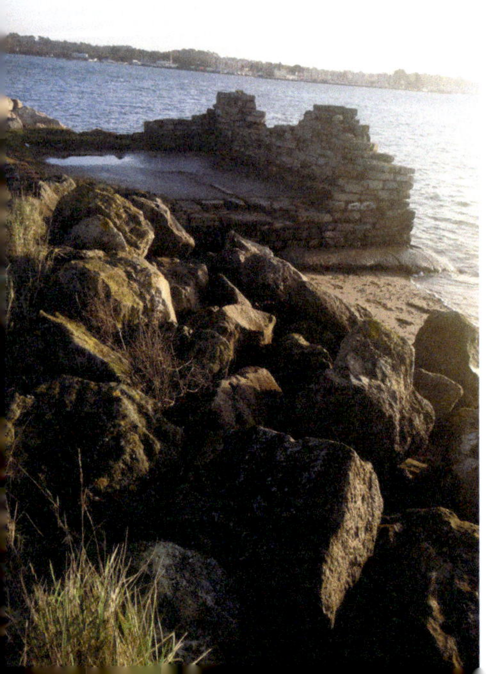

The remains of the Powder House.

The same building was used during the Second World War for ammunition storage, and was eventually demolished in 1963. Now there are only remnants of the building on the edge of the sea at Baiter.

Press Gangs

The alleyways leading from the Quay, behind the pubs and warehouses, were dark and forbidding, and ideal places for press gangs to lurk.

Many a Poole man enjoying a drink on the Quay in the time of Nelson's Navy would have awoken the next morning with a sore head, as they found themselves on the high seas, sailing off to fight the French as one of the Royal Navy's newest 'volunteers'. The

Below left and right: Some of the dark, forbidding alleyways still exist, although they are now somewhat sanitised in comparison to Nelson's days.

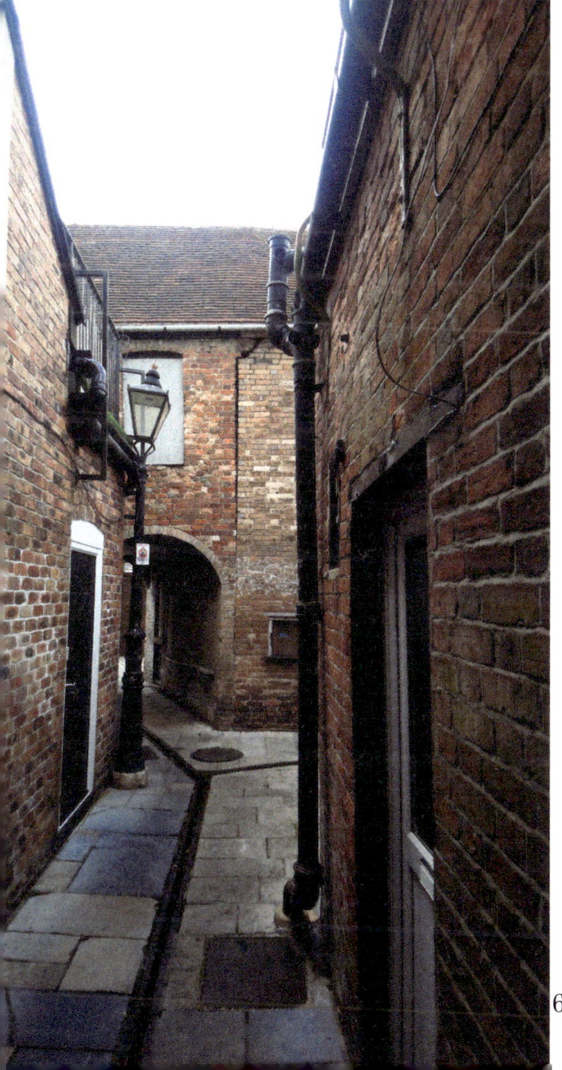
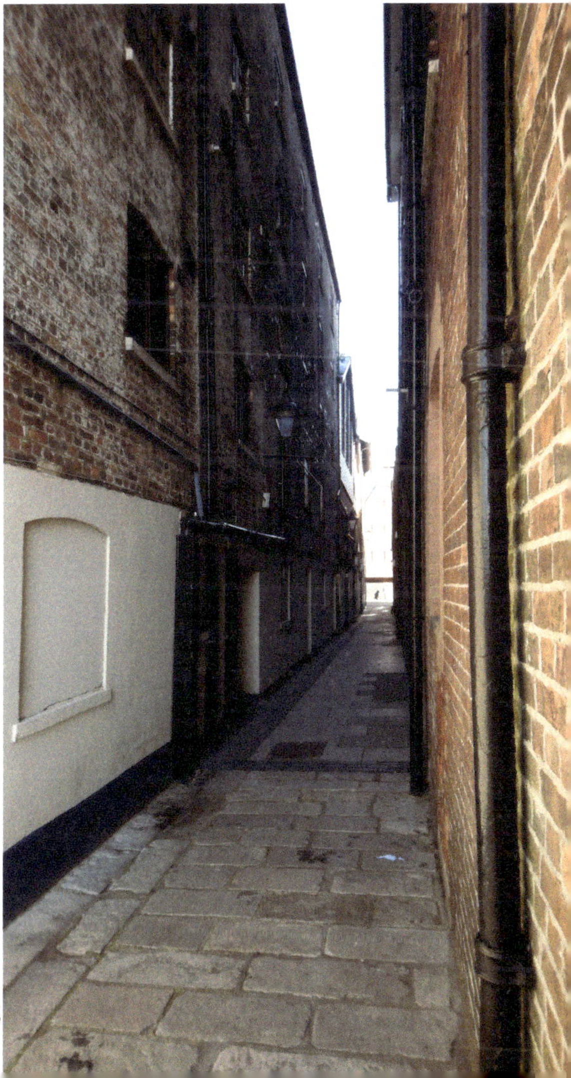

sore head was probably partially due to the alcohol, but in a larger measure due to being coshed on the back of it. Still, that was the least of their worries; they also had to start coming to terms with a diet of maggot-infested biscuits and regular floggings.

The press gangs were active during the American War of Independence (1775–83), when the French allied themselves with America. Later Britain was drawn into fighting the French Revolutionaries, and then shortly afterwards was involved in the Napoleonic Wars, which as far as naval engagements were concerned, finished at the Battle of Trafalgar in 1805. Throughout these times the press gangs ensured there were always plenty of men available for active service.

Poole of course was known to possess many experienced sailors from the fishing industry and Newfoundland trading, but the town didn't like to crow about this too much, for fear of attracting the attentions of the press gangs. Nevertheless, the press gangs were very much attracted to Poole, and they frequently pressed Poole mariners.

Quay and Old Town

The Quay and the adjoining Old Town have been the catalyst for the historical development of Poole since Iron Age people survived mainly on shellfish and crustaceans.

Later, transient Saxon fishermen developed an oyster fishery, which became apparent when the Quay area was reclaimed from the sea, and the Quay was subsequently built on a thick foundation of these shells. However, the first real settlers were Norman fishermen.

In medieval times, commodities for export, particularly wool, were funnelled into Poole from outlying areas of Dorset. Also, it was one of the few ports where merchants could dock, store their goods and display their wares. Consequently, Poole burgeoned from a small fishing village to become an important port.

The Quay.

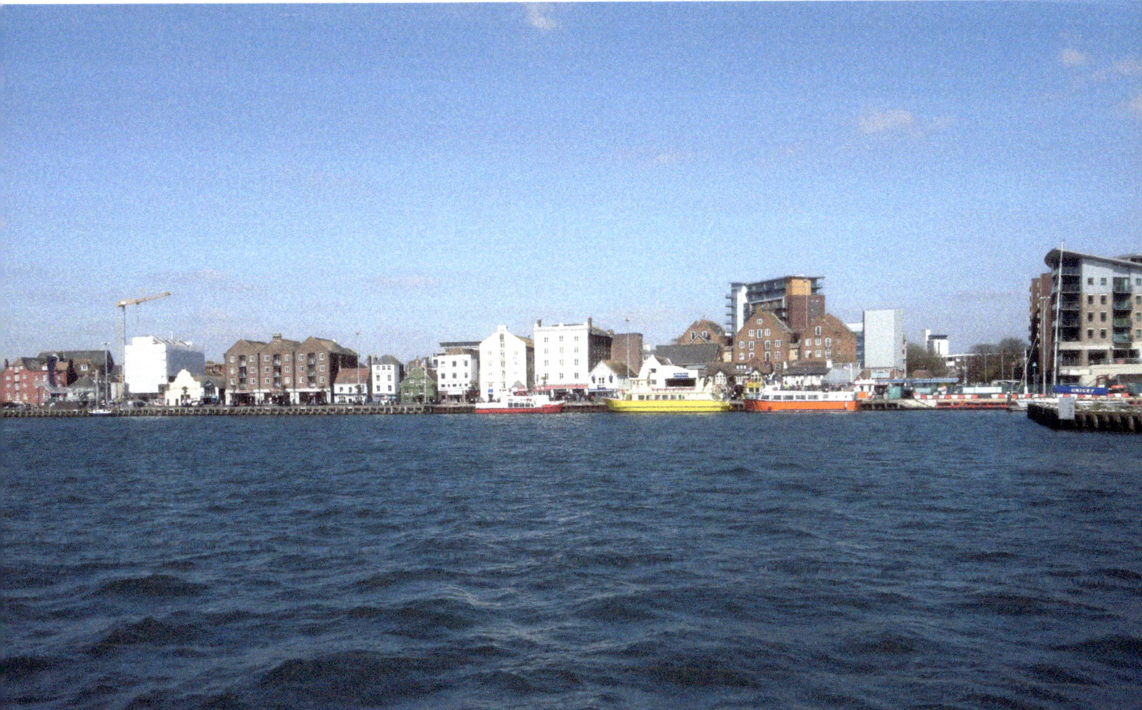

The Great Quay part of the Quay, around the Custom House, and the cobbled streets and alleyways behind it form the most historic part of the Quay and Old Town, with many of the buildings dating back to the fourteenth century. However, the overall style of the Old Town, which is a short way back from the Quay, is Georgian, as during the eighteenth century, wealthy merchants who had grown rich by trading in Newfoundland started building themselves some impressive mansions to signify their wealth and status.

In 1893–95, the town enlarged, and the Quay extended east, as industrial warehouses sprang up on this part of the Quay around Strand Street and Fish Street. This part of Poole is also considered to be Old Town, but was populated by seamen and industrial workers living in tenements, rather than wealthy merchants living in mansions. Very few old buildings remain, as they were destroyed in the slum clearances (see Slum Clearances).

Poole is still a working port, particularly on the Hamworthy side, where many gleaming Sunseeker yachts just off the production line can be seen adjacent to industrial cargo ships moored nearby. This side also includes a ferry terminal.

On the Poole side, the Fishermen's Dock nestles incongruously adjacent to a yachting marina which houses many luxurious vessels, most of which would have been built across the water at Sunseeker.

Rogers, Woodes

Woodes Rogers (1679–1732) is considered to be the man who discovered Robinson Crusoe. He was an accomplished seaman, privateer and circumnavigator who became the colonial governor of the Bahamas.

He was the son of a successful Poole Newfoundland merchant and spent his formative years in Poole, before his family moved to Bristol, where he became apprenticed to a sea captain.

In 1707, Rogers was approached by Captain William Dampier to take part in a privateering venture against the Spanish, with whom the British were at war.

Dampier was a friend of Rogers' father, and had recently been involved in a privateering expedition during which his crew mutinied. One of the crew members was a certain Scottish seaman by the name of Alexander Selkirk. He was cast adrift on a desert island after annoying Dampier by telling him the ship was likely to sink as the hull hadn't been properly protected against woodworm. Selkirk's fears were well founded, and he ended up with the better side of the arrangement, as the vessel did subsequently go down.

However, the 1707 Dampier and Rogers expedition, consisting of two ships, the *Duke* and *Duchess*, was far more successful, and in three years they circumnavigated the globe, and captured several ships. En route they pulled in to the remote Juan Fernandez Island, in order to stock up on lemons to prevent scurvy. This so happened to be the very island where Dampiers had abandoned Selkirk a few years earlier, and sure enough, they encountered a wild-looking Scotsman wearing goatskins and surviving off the land.

Selkirk didn't seem to have a problem with the fact that his former nemesis Dampier was the co-leader of the expedition and was just grateful to be rescued.

Some say that this was the inspiration for Daniel Defoe's *Robinson Crusoe*, as Rogers knew Defoe; whereas, others say that Defoe spoke to Selkirk himself in a Bristol pub, then called the Spyglass Inn, but now called the Llandoger Trow.

However, another possible inspiration for the story is that of Henry Pitman, a surgeon and Monmouth rebel who was transported to a Caribbean sugar plantation during the Bloody Assizes. He escaped in a rickety boat, which then became washed up on an uninhabited island. Eventually, he was picked up by a pirate ship and given passage to England in return for acting as a doctor onboard. He made it to England and was given a pardon in 1687.

Daniel Defoe himself was involved in the Monmouth Rebellion, escaping after the Battle of Sedgemoor and going into exile in Europe. He later returned to the south-west of England with William of Orange's army, before forging a very distinguished career in writing, the highlight of which was his book *Robinson Crusoe* based on either or both of these two characters.

Rolls, Samuel

The most impressive building in Poole High Street is called Beech Hurst, which is now the home of Jacobs and Reeves Solicitors. It was built in 1798, and was formerly the residence of Samuel Rolls, who was the main beneficiary of the estate of Joseph White, a wealthy Newfoundland merchant.

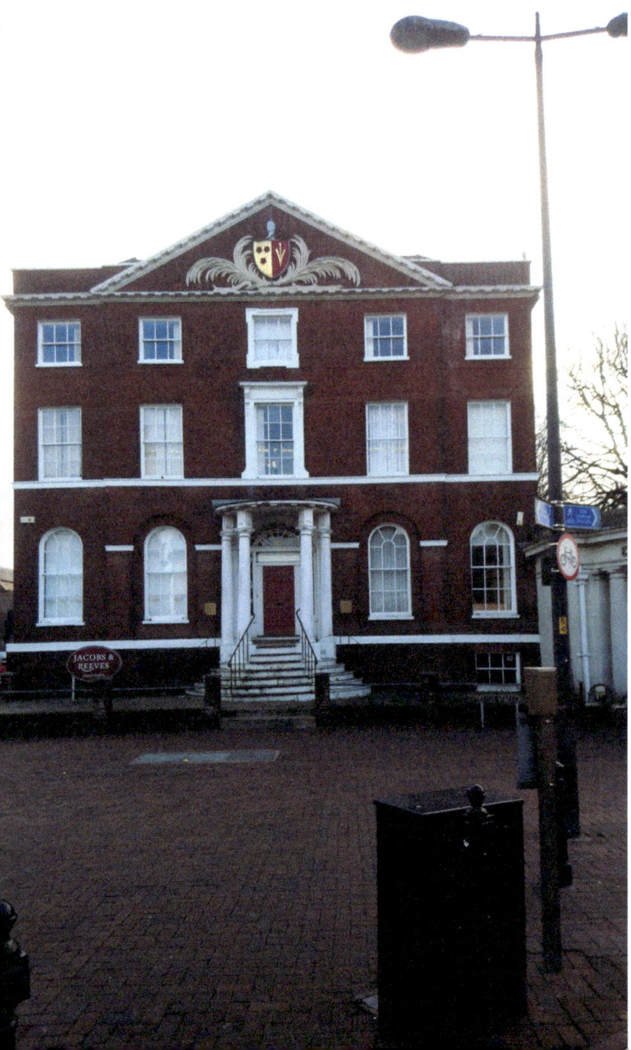

Beech Hurst.

The Rolls family coat of arms is prominently displayed, although Samuel Rolls only lived here for eleven years, before he died in 1809.

When the mansion was built it faced onto a swampy area known as Pitwines, later to become a gasworks and now Sainsbury's.

Royal Marines

The Royal Marines have had a base in Hamworthy, Poole, for many years. The base was built in 1942 as RAF Hamworthy, and used as a flying boat base (see Flying Boats).

In 1944, the base was handed over to the Royal Navy for use as a training centre for the D-Day landings, and was renamed HMS *Turtle*. The Royal Marines then took over the base in 1954, and at its peak in 1994, 600 Marines were based there, rising to peaks of a 1,000 during the build-up to operations.

In 1985, Margaret Thatcher visited the base to award battle honours and personally review the Royal Marines and Special Boat Squadron (SBS) in recognition of their contribution to the Falklands War, and in particular, the retaking of South Georgia and East Falkland. The Royal Marines were also awarded the Freedom of the Borough of Poole.

The pedestrianised square outside the Dolphin Shopping Centre has been named Falkland Square, and there is a memorial dedicated to all those who served their country in the Falklands War.

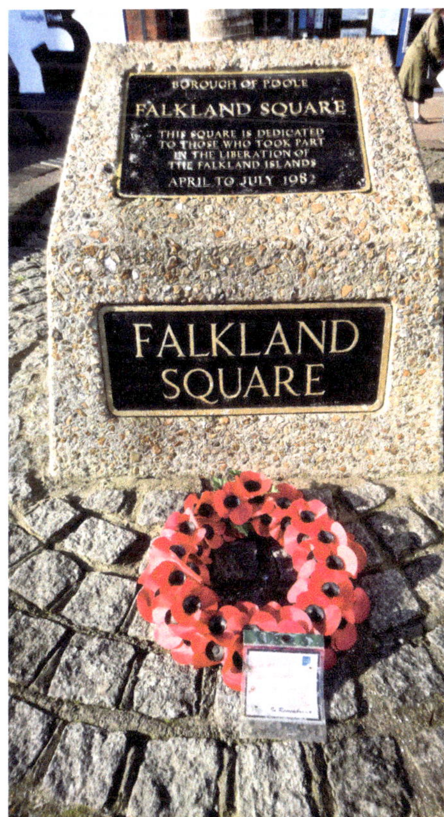

Falkland Square.

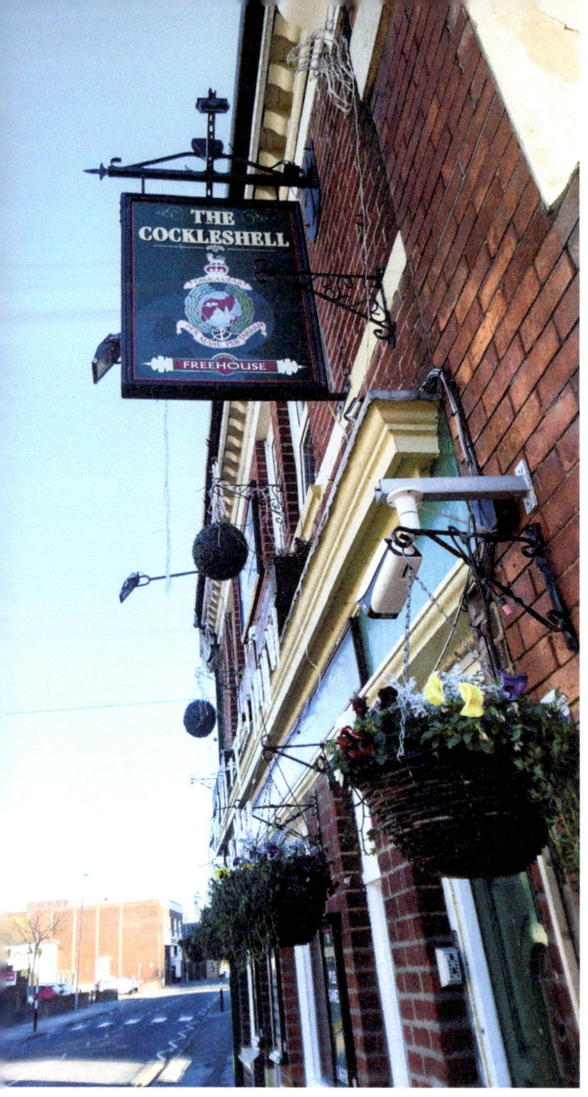

Cockleshell pub sign.

Today, there is still a Royal Marine presence in Hamworthy, and the Special Boat Squadron (SBS) have four squadrons based in Poole.

The Cockleshell pub in Lagland Street features a Royal Marines badge on the pub sign in recognition of the Cockleshell Heroes, who were ten Poole-based SBS Royal Marines who carried out a daring raid during the Second World War. The purpose of the raid was to disrupt German merchant shipping in the French port of Bordeaux, which the Royal Air Force had failed to accomplish despite repeated bombing attacks. The SBS achieved their aim by planting magnetic limpet mines on the hulls of the ships below the waterline.

Out of the ten men in five canoes who took part in the operation, only two survived. They evaded capture by travelling through occupied France, on to Spain and then Gibraltar.

The canoes they used for the raid were nicknamed cockleshells, as they folded up into the shape of a cockleshell. These were built in Poole and could be launched under water from a submarine. The training for this was carried out in Poole Bay.

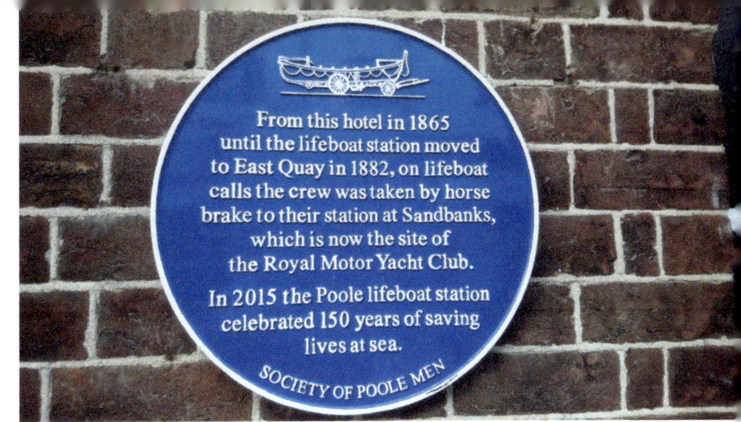

Plaque on the Antelope in recognition of Poole's first lifeboat crews.

Royal National Lifeboat Institution

The very first Poole lifeboat crews, which tended to consist of local fishermen, used the Antelope (see Antelope) as a mustering point from where they would then be transported by horse-drawn coach a distance of 5 miles to Sandbanks, where Poole's first lifeboat station was established in 1865. Sandbanks at this time wasn't the expensive real estate it is now, but was a desolate area of sand dunes. Fortunately, given the distance and the time involved in getting there, the lifeboat station was moved to the Quay in 1882 (see RNLI Museum).

RNLI Museum

Situated on the far reaches of the Eastern Quay next to Fishermen's Dock is the old lifeboat station, which is now a museum. It was built in 1882, and was in use until 1974, when it moved to Lilliput Marina. In 1988, the lifeboat station moved again, to its present site by the Lifting Bridge on the far western aspect of the Quay.

Old Lifeboat Station.

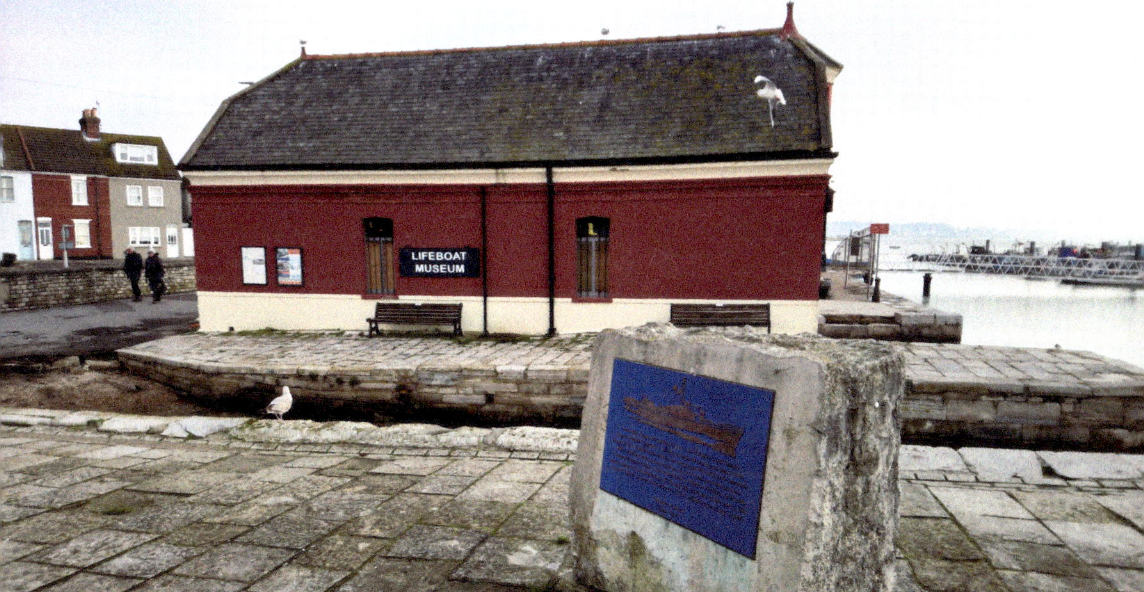

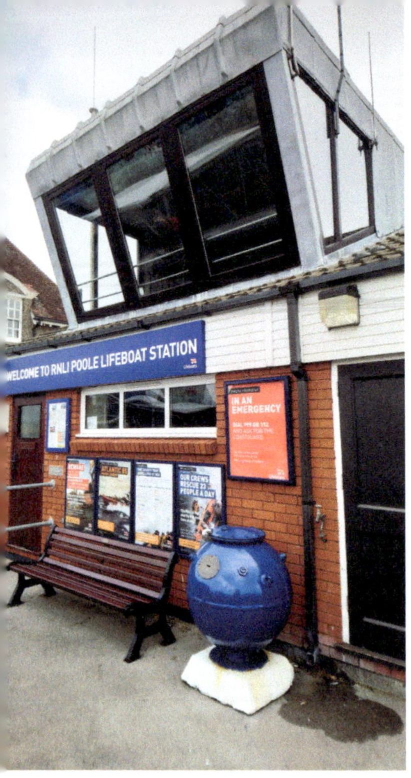

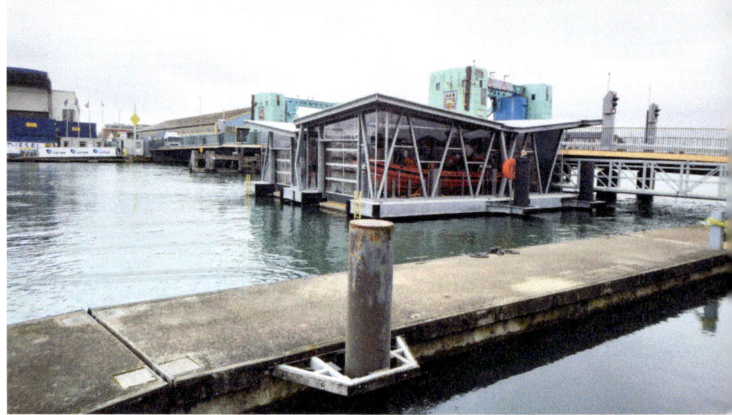

Above: Lifeboats in their pens ready for action.

Left: Operational Lifeboat Station.

Operational Lifeboat Station

Poole is the busiest lifeboat station in the country in terms of the number of call-outs. It covers Poole Harbour, which has 100 miles of shoreline, and includes Poole Bay, which has 7 miles of beaches from Sandbanks to Southbourne. These popular beaches result in a large number of call-outs involving holidaymakers and day-trippers.

The operational lifeboat station is situated on the western aspect of the Quay near the Lifting Bridge, and operates two inshore lifeboats, a B Class Atlantic 85 and a D class, which are launched from a boathouse almost underneath the bridge. There is also an all-weather Tyne-class lifeboat situated nearby.

RNLI Training College

Poole became the headquarters of the RNLI in the mid-1970s, and its offices house the administration and support staff.

The RNLI Training College, which was opened in 2004 by the Queen, is also based in Poole. It trains lifeboat crews and beach lifeguards from the whole of Great Britain and Ireland.

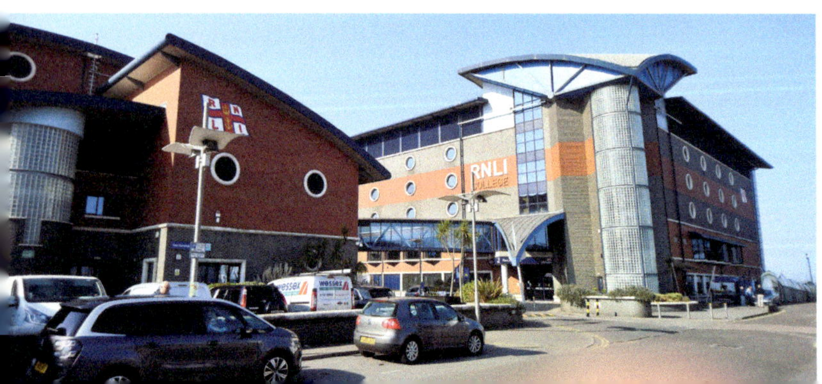

Part of the vast RNLI complex.

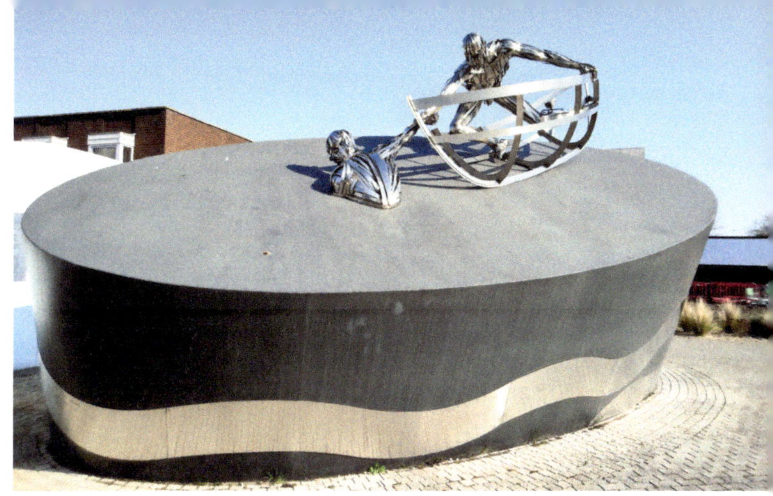

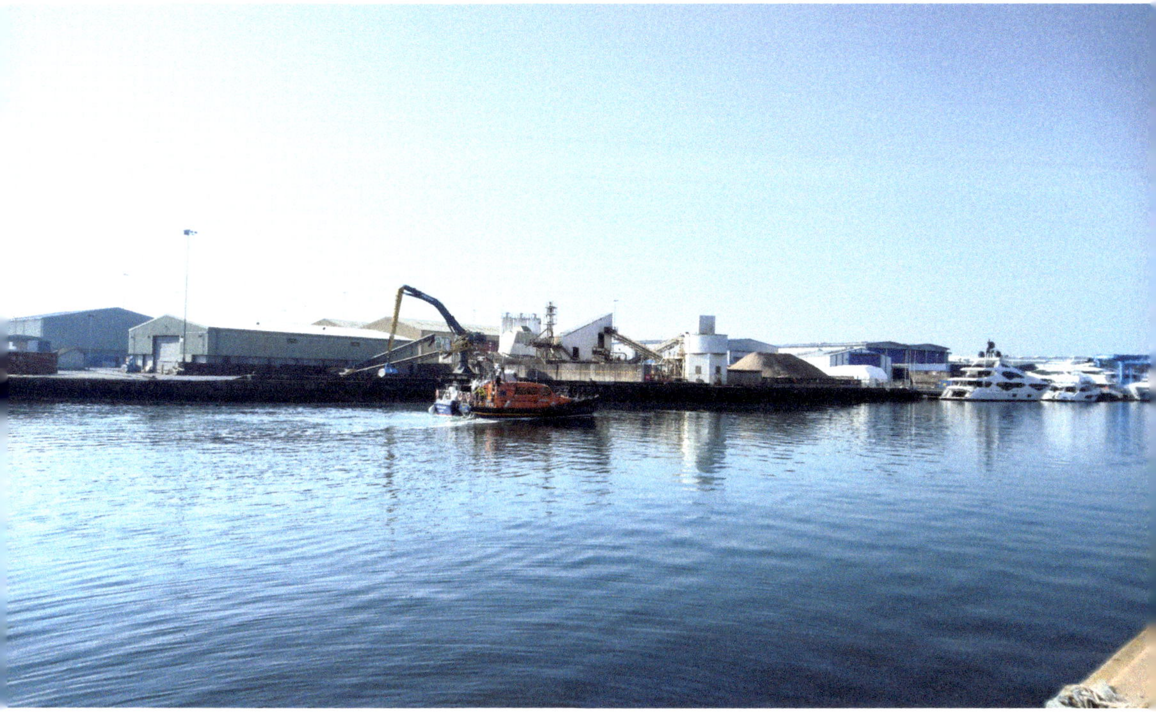

A later addition, in 2015, was the All Weather Lifeboat Centre, which boasts a sea survival pool where capsize drills can be practised, as well as drills concerning engine room fires and other emergencies. There is also a lifeboat bridge simulator, which simulates the dramatic conditions that lifeboat crews must regularly face at sea.

It is a frequent occurrence to see lifeboat crews from various parts of the country on training manoeuvres throughout the harbour.

RNLI Beach Lifeguards

There are fourteen RNLI lifeguarded beaches covering a 7-mile stretch from Sandbanks to Southbourne, which are patrolled by beach lifeguards on a seasonal basis.

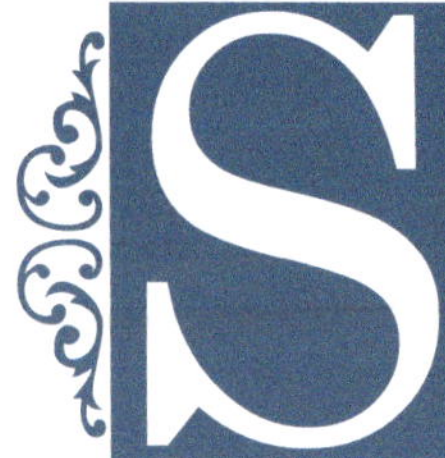

Scaplen's Court

Scaplen's Court is situated between the King's Head and Poole Museum, on the corner of Lower High Street and Sarum Street, and only came to light in 1923, after the damage from a storm revealed a medieval building hiding underneath a 9-inch layer of brick.

It is a Grade I listed building, built from local Purbeck stone, dating back to the fourteenth century. It is believed to have been built as a house for a rich merchant and then developed into a courtyard inn.

It is considered to be Poole's most complete medieval domestic building, although some historians suggest it was Poole's first Guildhall. Merchants would have stayed here, and also pilgrims who sailed from Poole to the shrine of Santiago de Compostela in Northern Spain (see Coat of Arms).

In 1598, a rich widow called Alice Green owned the property, and she lived with her maid, Agnes Beard. Agnes was murdered in the house, and it is said that her apron-clad ghost still haunts the building. Other resident ghostly figures include a bearded man wearing a long black coat. Another figure has been seen wearing a bowler hat, and in fact a ghostly image of this gentleman was apparently caught on CCTV camera in 2008.

In the seventeenth century, it was known as the George Inn, and provided lodgings for the Roundheads during the Civil War, as evidenced by some graffiti found on the

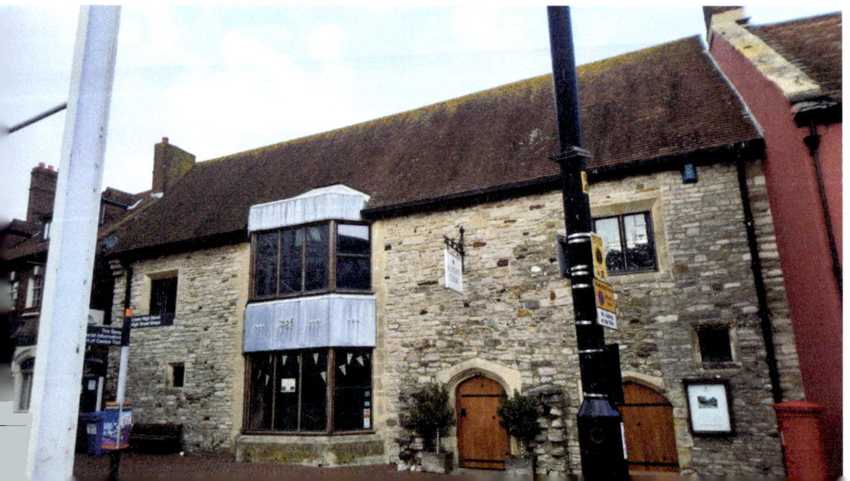

Scaplen's Court.

walls. It is next door to the King's Head, which in those days was called the Plume of Feathers (see King's Head).

Poole supported the Roundheads, mainly because the merchants were against the ship money tax imposed by Charles I, and were not very happy with the lack of protection from pirates afforded by the Crown (see Newfoundland Trade and Poole Pirates and Privateers).

After the George Inn closed in the eighteenth century, the house was acquired by a prosperous cabinetmaker by the name of John Scaplen. During the Victorian period, Scaplen's Court went into decline, and was threatened with demolition.

In 1927, the Society of Poole bought the house and undertook renovations, during which a shilling was found dating back to the reign of Mary I in the fourteenth century. Coins or tokens dating back to the reign of King Charles II in the seventeenth century have also been found, and local historians believe that the George Inn issued its own beer tokens.

The building was then opened to the public in 1929, and then in 1930, the 'Old World Garden' was laid out to a design donated by George Dillistone, 'Garden Architect of Tunbridge Wells'.

The building was further restored in 1986 and is now used as an education centre, which is part of Poole Museum. It contains a Victorian schoolroom and kitchen and is open to the public during the month of August.

In 2000, the garden was turned into a herb and physic garden by volunteers, and contains plants traditionally associated with healing.

Slum Clearances

After the boom years of the Newfoundland trade, Poole suffered from an economic slump throughout most of the nineteenth century. This was further compounded by the unemployment and poverty that were nationwide problems in the 1920s and '30s.

The labyrinth of narrow backstreets and alleyways leading from the Eastern Quay into the Old Town were overcrowded, damp, rat-infested slums, and during the 1920s and '30s, this quarter was also dominated by an enormous gasworks, which added to the general misery, as the whole area was shrouded in coal dust and had an accompanying sound of clanking machinery.

However, in the decades after the war, many major national companies were attracted to the town, resulting in 10,000 more homes being built between 1946 and 1966.

A major slum clearance scheme was also taking place during the same period, as over 1,000 condemned homes, mainly in the Eastern Old Town area around Strand Street, Castle Street, East Street, Lagland Street and South Road, were demolished, as Poole Council managed to succeed where the Luftwaffe had failed and destroyed the tenements and dwellings that had seen people through two World Wars.

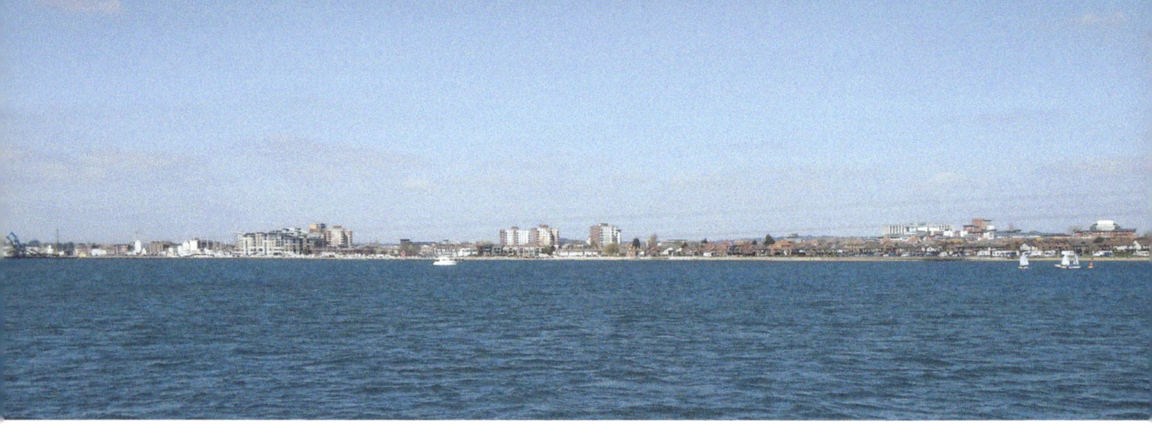

Poole's four distinctive tower blocks.

The occupants were rehoused by the council as these dwellings were replaced with four tower blocks, and a further two were built close to the town centre in Sterte.

Most of the buildings that were demolished dated back to before 1850, and some say that much of Poole's medieval architectural heritage was also destroyed.

Smuggling

By the late seventeenth century, piracy was abating, but a new unlawful trade of smuggling was becoming widespread. In the sixteenth, seventeenth, eighteenth and nineteenth centuries, peaking between 1770 and 1815, Poole's coastline abounded with smugglers, mainly due to the ideal prerequisites of a long shoreline and numerous inlets.

There were mitigating factors to these activities, as it was a time when high taxes were sought to finance wars. Also, the imposition of duty on imported goods significantly raised prices beyond the pocket of many.

Pub landlords would frequently use barrels of wine, Madeira, sherry and port that had been stamped as having duty paid, and then refill them with smuggled liquor.

In 1804, smugglers were so prolific in Poole that customs officials estimated that 120,000 gallons of liquor on which duty had not been paid was coming in.

By the 1850s, the effect of the return of peace after the Napoleonic Wars, along with more efficient customs and tax reductions all but destroyed the practice. Another factor in the decline of smuggling was the introduction of the coastguard in the 1820s, which increased the risk of being caught.

Notorious Poole Smugglers

Robert Bennett

Robert Bennett was the innkeeper at the George Inn and used the premises to store tobacco, which he would claim was sea damaged in order to avoid paying tax on it. The George Inn is now Scaplen's Court and is one of the finest examples of a fourteenth-century town house on the south coast (see Scaplen's Court).

John Carter

John Carter was the head of a violent smuggling gang. He led a double life as a legitimate merchant who owned many businesses, and unbelievably was mayor of Poole from 1676 to 1681, 1699 and 1705. His businesses provided numerous hiding places and outlets for the contraband.

Corrupt Customs Officials

In the late seventeenth century, Poole Custom House was under the command of an alcoholic by the name of Dudley Hopper, who spent most of his working hours inebriated. This enabled one of his officials, Thomas Barney, to frequently take advantage by accepting payment to allow certain goods ashore. Another Poole customs man was dismissed as he was found to be in league with the Carter gang.

Isaac Gulliver

Isaac Gulliver (1745–1822) was Dorset's most celebrated and successful smuggler. Although, he was actually born in Wiltshire, he lived the majority of his life in Kinson, which was originally in the Borough of Poole but is now in the Borough of Bournemouth. There used to be a pub in Kinson called Gulliver's Travels.

He was a wanted man after his involvement in a clash with customs officers between Bournemouth and Poole, but regularly evaded their attention.

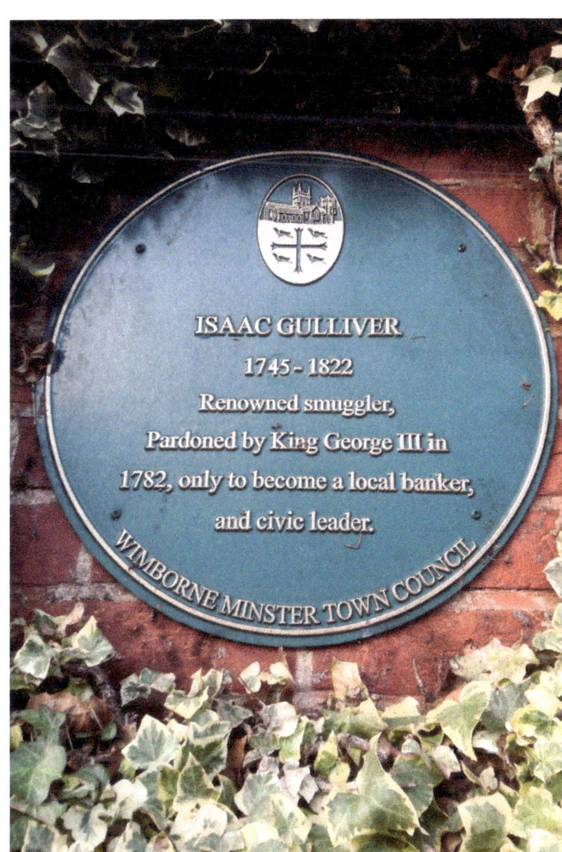

A plaque on Isaac Gulliver's House.

On one occasion, he was secreted out of the King's Head, hidden inside a barrel, under the very noses of customs officials. On another occasion, he eluded customs men by lying motionless in a coffin with his face covered with white powder as he played dead.

He controlled a massive smuggling operation which spread its tentacles across the whole of Dorset and into Devon, Wiltshire and Hampshire, but having amassed a tidy fortune, he retired from smuggling and was given a King's Pardon by George III. He then became a wine merchant (although it was believed that a large proportion of his wine was of the smuggled variety), banker and civic leader in Wimborne, and upon his death was buried in the vault of Wimborne Minster.

Although, he was a powerfully built man, he was considered a gentleman, and it is claimed his pistol, which now resides in the Russell-Cotes Museum in Bournemouth, was never used.

There is an area in Poole where Isaac Gulliver plied his trade which was formerly called Salterns but was renamed Lilliput. Many believe the name change refers to the well-known book *Gulliver's Travels* by Jonathan Swift, in which Gulliver, a sea captain, travels to a land called Lilliput.

Robert Trotman

Robert Trotman is buried in St Andrew's Churchyard, Kinson. He was shot in 1765 during a fierce battle with customs men who found twenty smugglers loading a consignment of tea on the shore between Poole and Bournemouth. The inscription on his headstone reads:

> Robert Trotman, barbarously murdere'd by the Revenue 1765:
>
> A little tea one leaf I did not steal.
> For guiltless blood shed. I to God appeal.
> Put tea in one scale, human Blood in t'other.
> And think what tis to slay thy harmless Brother.

Swash Channel Wreck

The Swash Channel wreck was discovered in the 1990s in the approach to Poole Harbour. It is the remains of a seventeenth-century, high-status, Dutch merchant ship called *The Fame*, which is believed to have come to grief whilst bound for the tropics.

The site was designated as a protected historic wreck in 2004 and is now administered by Historic England.

In 2006, Bournemouth University students become involved in what is the largest underwater excavation since the *Mary Rose*, and have brought up over 1,000 artefacts including pottery, barrels, personal items, an iron cannon, and a 28-foot rudder with a face carved onto it.

Twin Sails Bridge

The Twin Sails Bridge provides a second road link from Poole Town Centre to Hamworthy, and works in conjunction with the Lifting Bridge on Poole Quay (see Lifting Bridge).

The bridge was opened in March 2012 by Princess Anne, and then to traffic in April 2012. It was the first bridge of its type to be built in the world, and the unique twin sails structure reflects Poole's proud maritime heritage.

Unfortunately, it has had a few teething problems, which have forced closures for more than a total of six months, and so far up to and including 2019 has cost Poole Borough Council a total of thirteen million pounds to keep operational.

The Twin Sails Bridge.

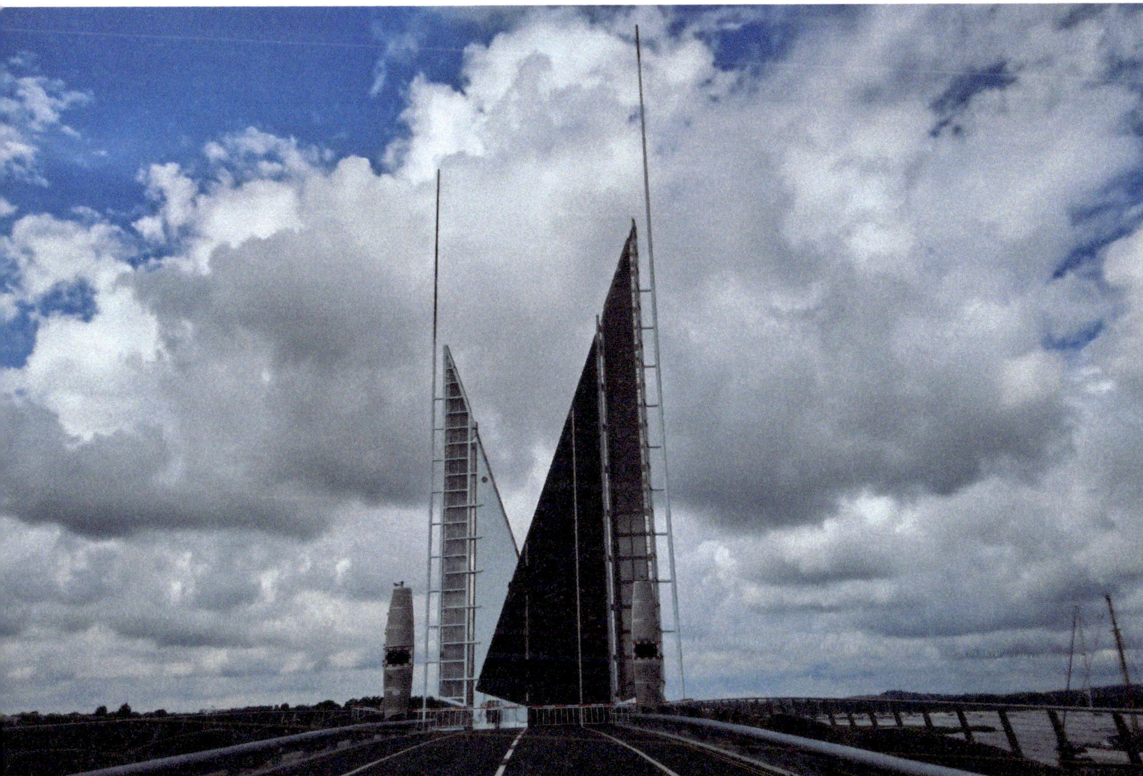

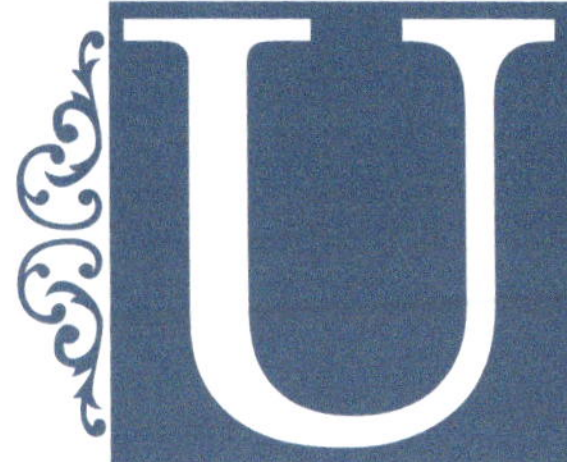

Undying Love

The King Charles is believed by many to be the most haunted pub in Dorset, although other Poole pub landlords would not necessarily agree.

One particularly sad story relates to a former landlady and sailor who fell in love and had agreed to marry upon the sailor's return. On the day he was due back, she waited anxiously whilst looking despondently out to sea, fearing that he had perished in the terrible storm that was pounding the harbour and surrounding area that day. Believing the worst when he failed to arrive, she slung a rope over a beam and hanged herself.

The following day, the sailor did return and found the limp body of his intended hanging from the beam. He cut her down, but then in a fit of despair turned the knife on himself, stabbing himself through the heart.

The haunting takes the form of bottles and glasses smashing for no reason, heavy footsteps being heard on the stairs in the middle of the night, doors slamming, and a shadowy figure has been seen dressed in black looking out to sea. Also, visitors have

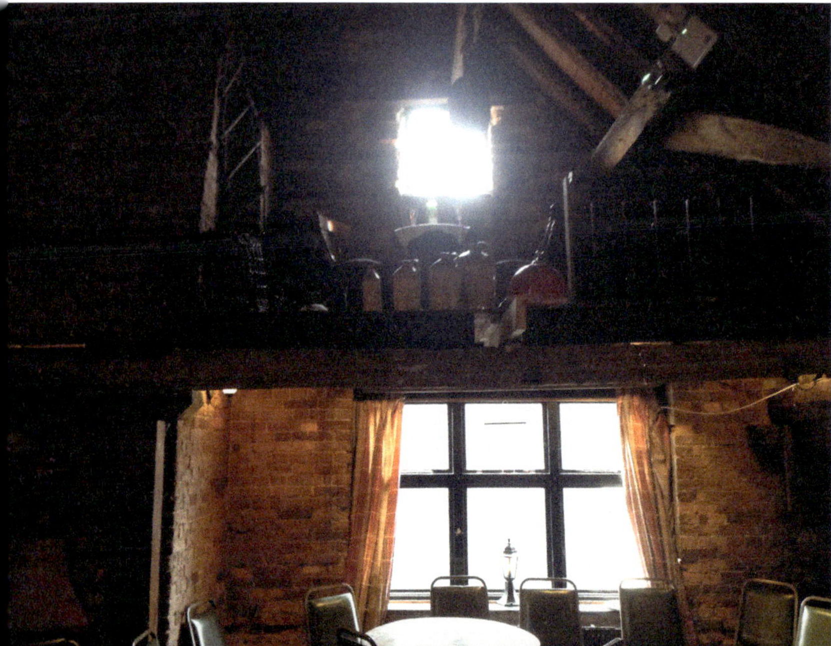

The window through which the former landlady kept a constant vigil, looking out to sea in search of her sweetheart. See the table and chairs set out for the ghost's benefit on the upper landing.

been nudged or tapped, only to find no one there. Some even say they've heard the faint cries of a female voice saying, 'help me, help me'.

Other spirits who are said to be at large in the pub are a laughing fisherman and a ghost of a little girl.

Upton House

The land for this house was acquired at Upton, just outside central Poole, by William Spurrier, four times mayor of Poole, whose wealth was gained from the Newfoundland trade.

The house was built by his son Christopher between 1816 and 1818, and its west wing was added in 1825. However, the decline of the Newfoundland trade, coupled with Christopher's gambling, forced him to sell the property in 1825 to Sir Edward Doughty, a member of the Tichborne family.

Upton House remained within the Tichborne family until 1901, when spiralling debts resulted in the necessity of a sale to the Lewellins. They held it until 1957, when it was bequeathed to the Borough of Poole, who then rented it for several years to Prince Carol of Romania.

However, in 1976, public opinion decreed that the estate should be opened as a country park for the benefit of the people of Poole, and eventually in 1981, its doors opened to the public.

In 2015, Upton Country Park became part of the newly established Holes Bay Nature Park, and now features an area of bird hides.

The north aisle of St James' Church also houses an early nineteenth-century monument to William Spurrier.

Upton House.

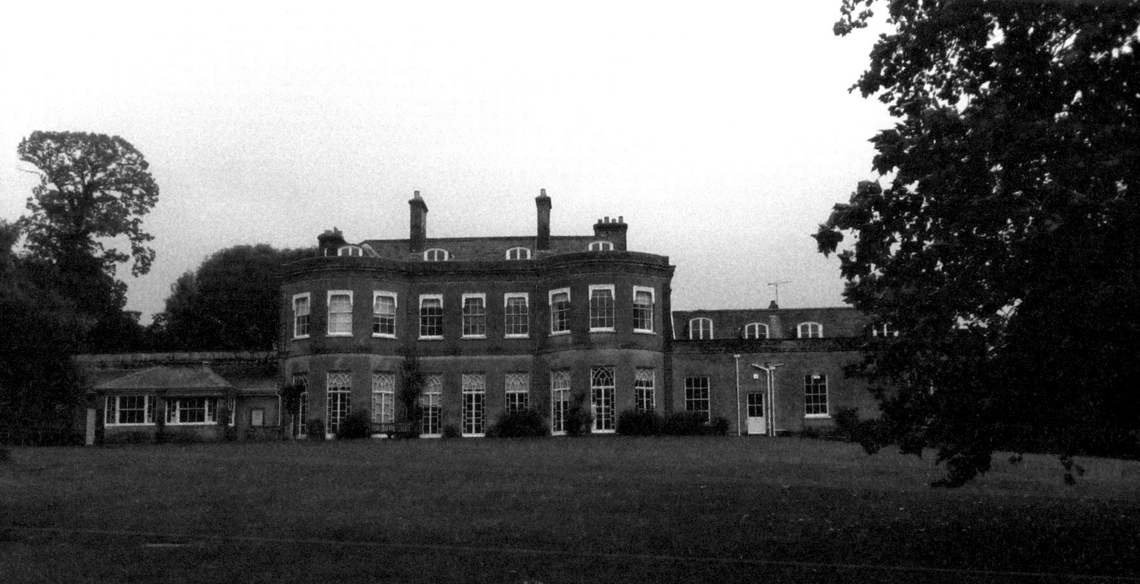

Vice

In the seventeenth and eighteenth centuries the ladies of the night were frequently hauled before the courts, where their punishments would include such delights as a day in the stocks or being ducked on the ducking stool. However, by the early nineteenth century, as the port expanded, prostitution was flourishing even more.

Later in the early twentieth century, Black Bess and Cockle Kate were two foul-mouthed prostitutes who, in spite of being banned from every pub in Poole, still plied their trade with alacrity. They were popular with sailors, fishermen and dockers alike, despite their tendency to pick their clients' pockets.

Black Bess was said to be slim, dark and attractive; whereas Cockle Kate, who, as her name implied, was also a hawker of cockles and whelks, was somewhat overweight, and used vocabulary that would strip paint at a hundred yards.

Viking

During the late 1980s and 1990s the Viking was a highly insalubrious establishment situated on the Quay front, at the top of one of the former warehouses, above the old aquarium and reptile house. It could loosely be termed as a nightclub, although, in reality, it was more of a place to continue drinking after the pubs had shut.

The queue to get in extended up a long, winding staircase, where drunks would frequently tap on the glass cages of snakes and various other reptiles for entertainment value.

It was laughably a members' club, although females never had a problem getting in, regardless of whether they were members or not. For the male of the species, options included claiming you had left your membership card on the bus, or other such lame excuses. I suppose it would have been easier to just become a member, but it never seemed such a good idea when sober.

Vital Statistics

Two of Great Britain's five Miss World winners were from Poole – Anne Sidney in 1964 and Sarah-Jane Hutt in 1983. Both attended Parkstone Grammar School; so its official, Poole has the most beautiful women in the world.

Wesley

The Restoration of the Monarchy in the form of Charles II after the Civil War (1642–51) also involved the restoration of the Church of England, as opposed to Cromwell's more puritanical version of the Protestant religion.

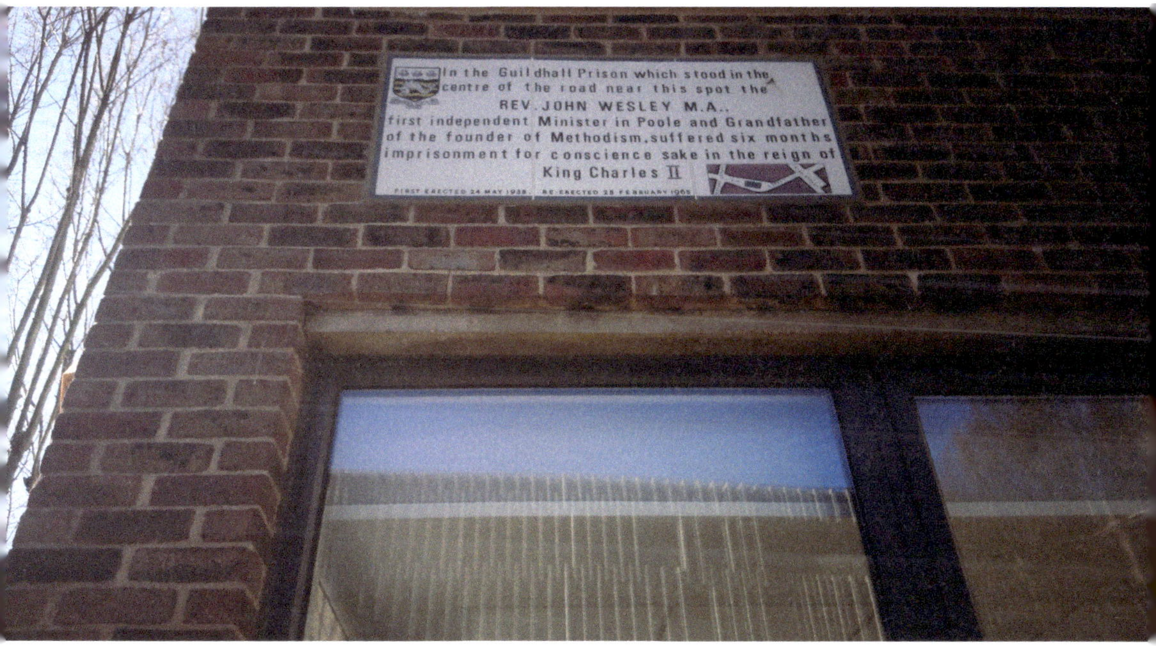

Above: Plaque showing the site where John Wesley was imprisoned.

Right: United Reform Church, Skinner Street.

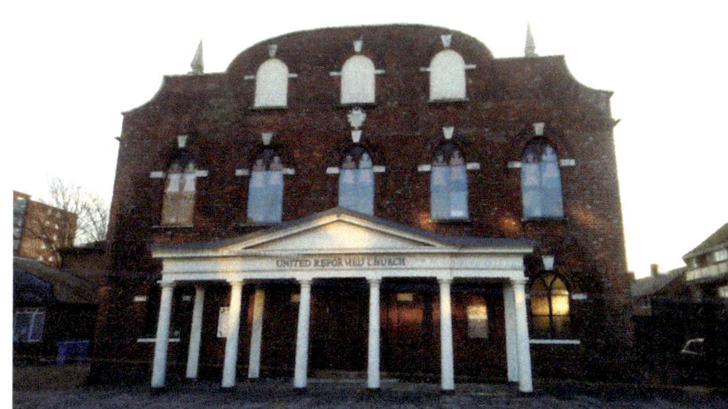

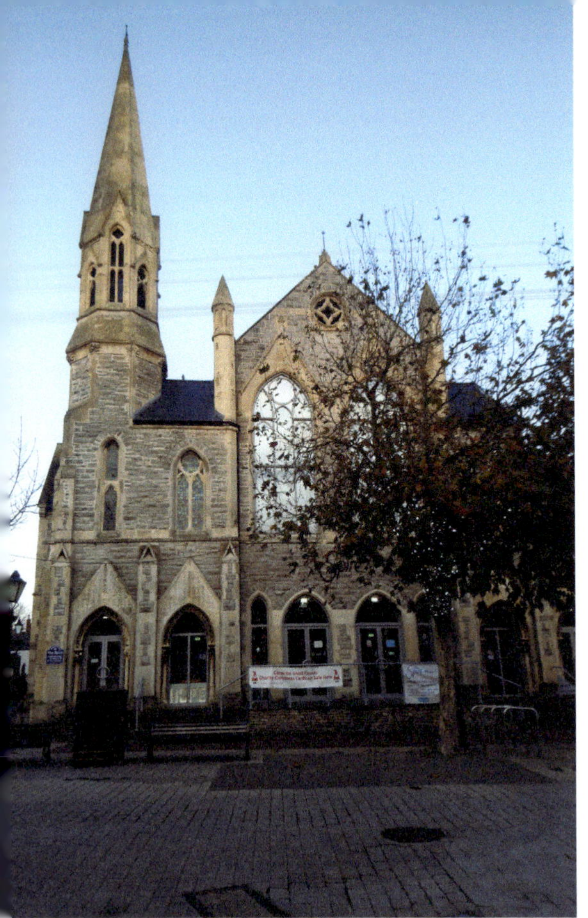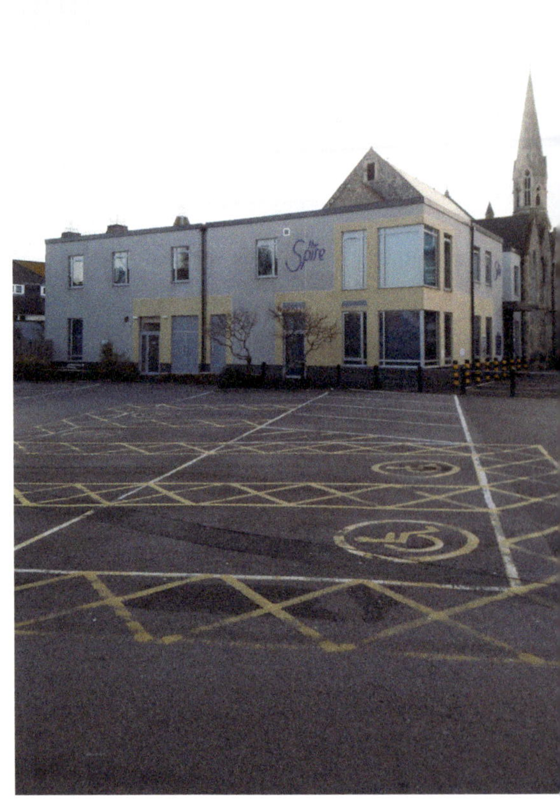

Above left: The Spire Church.

Above right: The Spire Church, complete with the new carbuncle of an annex. How bad must the winning entry of the Carbuncle Cup have been for this not to have taken the trophy?

Many preferred the more puritanical strain, and these people were known as Nonconformists. Dorset in general was a hotbed of religious nonconformism and Poole was no exception.

The 'Cavalier Parliament' of Charles II, which was elected in 1661, wanted to punish the Puritans in revenge for the Civil War, and for imposing their way of life on the nation. Accordingly, an Act of Uniformity was initiated, which required all clergy to accept the prescribed Book of Common Prayer and not deviate from that.

John Wesley was the vicar at Winterbourne Whitchurch in Dorset from 1658 to 1662. He was banned for praising Cromwell and criticizing the king, thus contravening the 1662 Act.

Shortly afterwards, a group of nonconformists in Poole approached Wesley and asked if he would be their pastor. He was happy to oblige, and it is believed they held their secret meetings in Hill Street, until Wesley was eventually discovered and imprisoned in Poole for six months.

After Wesley's death in 1678, nonconformism in Poole continued to flourish, and meanwhile, John Wesley's grandsons, one of whom was also named John, and the other, Charles Wesley, went on to become the founders of Methodism in 1729.

Later in 1777, a Methodist church was established in Skinner Street, Poole, called the United Reform Church. It was renovated in the 1880s but is Poole's oldest surviving church building and is Grade II listed.

A new Methodist church was then built in Poole by Charles Bell in the late 1800s from Purbeck and Bath stone. Its spire was the tallest structure in Poole, and was a landmark for mariners.

Many years later in 2016, an annex was added to the rear of the church, which was not exactly of an imaginative design. In fact, it was nominated for the Carbuncle Cup, which is an accolade given to the ugliest building in Britain.

The pulpit of the spire church is a memorial to Revd J. Wesley, the grandfather of the founder of Methodism, and the not-for-profit café attached to the church is called Wesley's.

West End House

West End House was built in the early eighteenth century for John Slade, who was a wealthy Newfoundland merchant. It is a Grade II listed building and a prime example of early Georgian architecture. It dominates St James' Square and overlooks St James' Church in the Old Town quarter. The four stone salt urns and pineapples on top of the façade allude to the source of the family's wealth.

In the nineteenth century the house was owned by Jessie Carter, the founder of Poole Pottery.

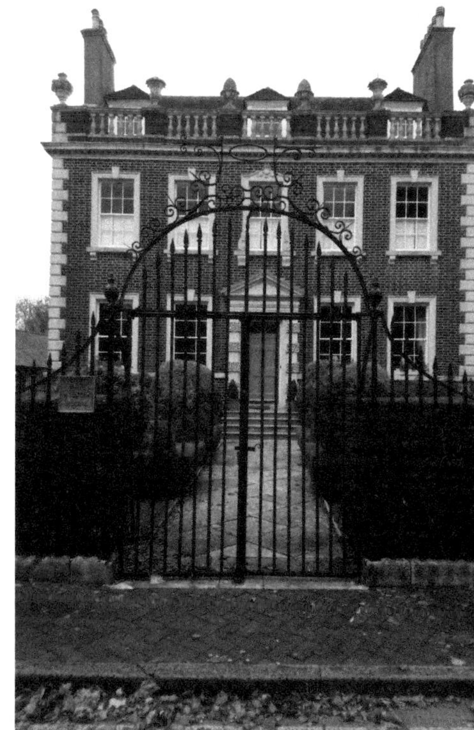

West End House.

Wimborne – Lord

Sir John Guest was a Welsh engineer and entrepreneur who had made a fortune from a steelworks in South Wales.

Sir John and Lady Charlotte Guest purchased the Canford Manor Estate in 1846 (now Canford School), thus becoming the Lord and Lady of the Manor. They had a son, Ivor Guest.

Ivor married in 1902, and he and his wife Cornelia were given the title of the First Lord and Lady Wimborne.

The town greatly benefitted from their alliance as they had a very philanthropic outlook. They initially opened a small hospice for the poor in West Street, but later, Lady Wimborne persuaded her husband to open Cornelia Hospital in Longfleet Road in 1907. This was renamed Poole General Hospital in 1948, and now forms part of Poole Hospital NHS Foundation Trust.

In another great act of benevolence, they donated two areas of land to the people of Poole, in the form of Poole Park and Parkstone Park, now called Ashley Cross Green. Poole Park was opened in 1890 by the Prince of Wales, later to become Edward VII, who stayed at Canford Manor the night before as a guest of Lord and Lady Wimborne.

The park became known as the people's park as it could be enjoyed by everyone, and in 2015 it celebrated its 125th anniversary. Today the park boasts facilities for cricket, parkrun, windsurfing, sailing, paddle boating, rowing, boating, kayaking, tennis, two children's playgrounds, indoor ice skating, a children's ball pool, crazy golf, bowling green, a miniature railway, model boating, a café and a restaurant where you can watch ducks, swans and geese in both instances. Plus anything else you can think of to do on a large expanse of grass such as playing football or enjoying a picnic.

Lord Wimborne.

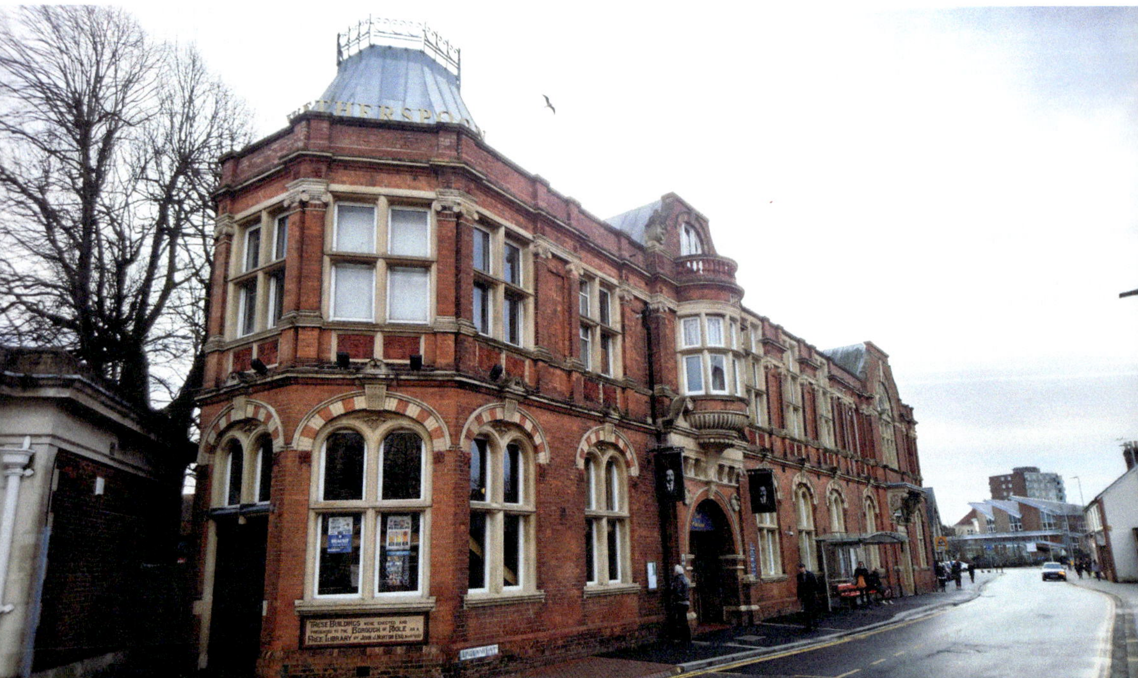

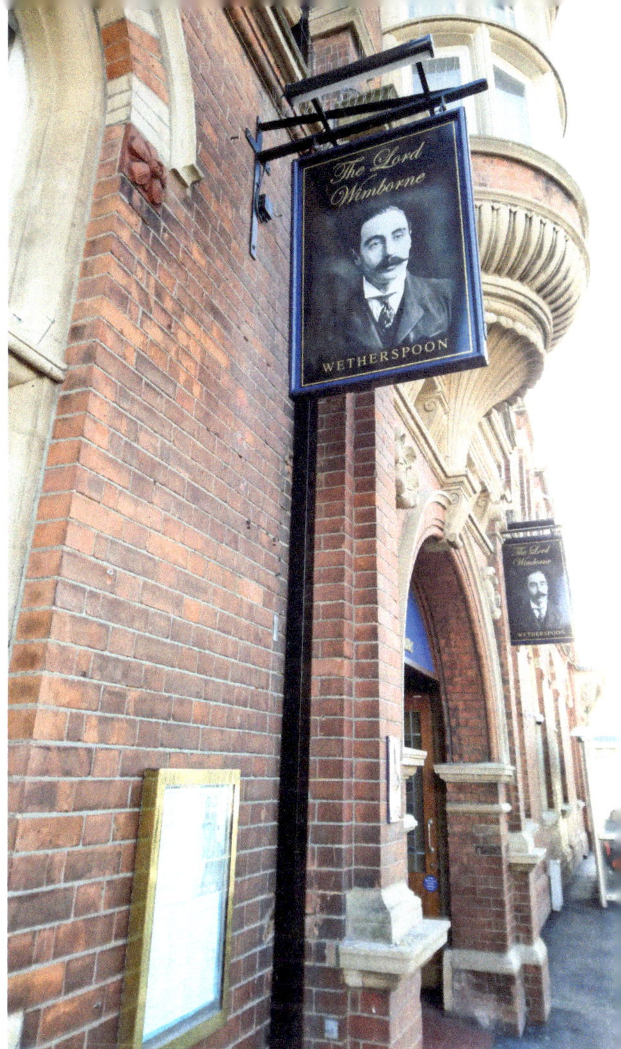

Lord Wimborne pub sign.

Lord and Lady Wimborne made a further contribution for the benefit of the town when in 1887 they donated land to be used for the benefit of the townspeople, as a way of recognising Queen Victoria's Golden Jubilee. Alderman John Norton, a timber merchant, suggested a free public library and agreed to meet the cost of building it.

Lord Wimborne was elected Lord Mayor in 1896, in recognition of the great contribution he had made to the town.

In 2002, the Lord Wimborne, a Wetherspoon's pub, opened at the site that had previously been the town public library. Alderman Norton would surely be turning in his grave if he could see the current use of the building, as he was a devout teetotaler.

Wool House or Town Cellars

Poole prospered during the twelfth century due to trade with Bordeaux in France, which at the time belonged to the English Crown. This allowed Poole to overhaul Wareham as the premier port and major town in the area, and become Dorset's Port of Staple, which meant it was licensed to import and export staple commodities – mainly wool and leather produced in the outlying areas of rural Dorset.

The building that was used to store those commodities was the Wool House/Town Cellars, which was built in 1350 and stands at the junction of Thames Street and the Quay, adjacent to the Custom House. It is considered to be one of the most important surviving medieval port buildings in northern Europe, and the finest surviving example of a wool house in England. It was originally a much larger building, but was divided in two in the 1780s, to allow access to the High Street, and thus the main route inland from the Quay (see King Charles).

It is part of this original building which is now part of the King Charles pub. The other, larger section now hosts the Local History Centre, which is part of Poole Museum and is just behind the Custom House. The building we see today is a fifteenth-century structure, but this overlies an even older structure dating back to 1350.

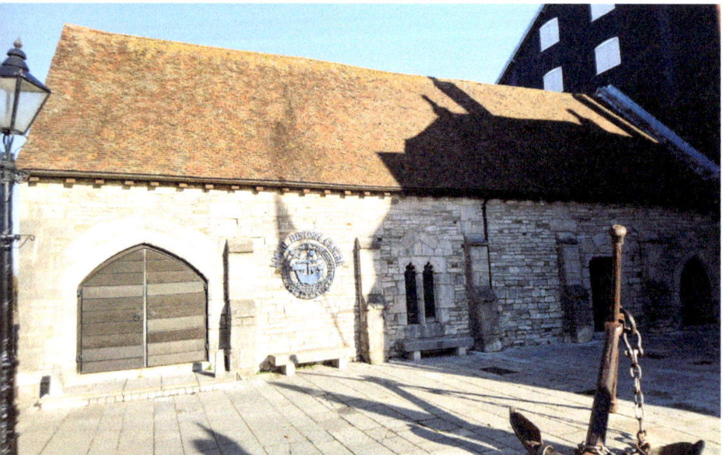

Left: The Wool House.

Below: The view from the quayside aspect, showing Thames Street cutting between the Local History Centre and the Kings Hall part of the King Charles. In medieval times these were one building known as the Wool House or Town Cellars, before Thames Street was cut through them. To the right as you look at the picture is the Custom House and to the left is the Harbour Office.

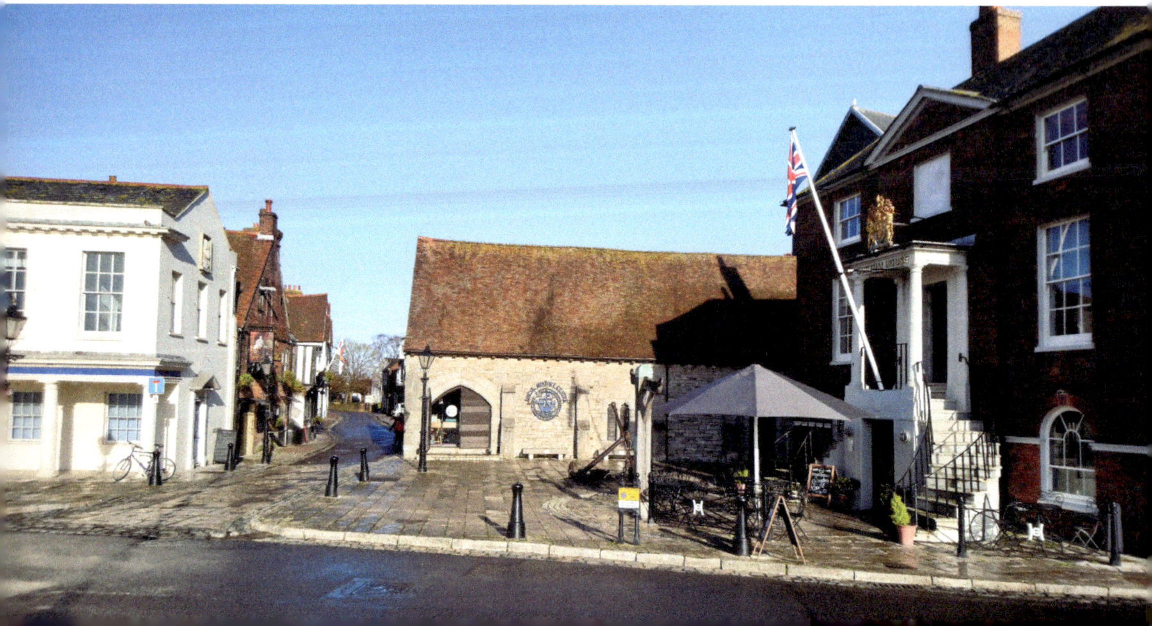

Xmas

Poole, like every other town in Britain, has its fair share of Christmas events. The Dolphin Centre often features a Santa's grotto, complete with Santa and attendant elves, and of course there is always a panto at the Lighthouse.

Santa usually arrives at the Quay, before being transported by sleigh, led by various marching bands, to Falkland Square just outside the Dolphin Centre where potential shoppers are conveniently deposited. Another occasion involves Santa arriving by boat at the Quay, where he sets up camp in a grotto.

Genial and charismatic local resident Mr Harry Redknapp turns on the lights, and adds an instant feel-good factor.

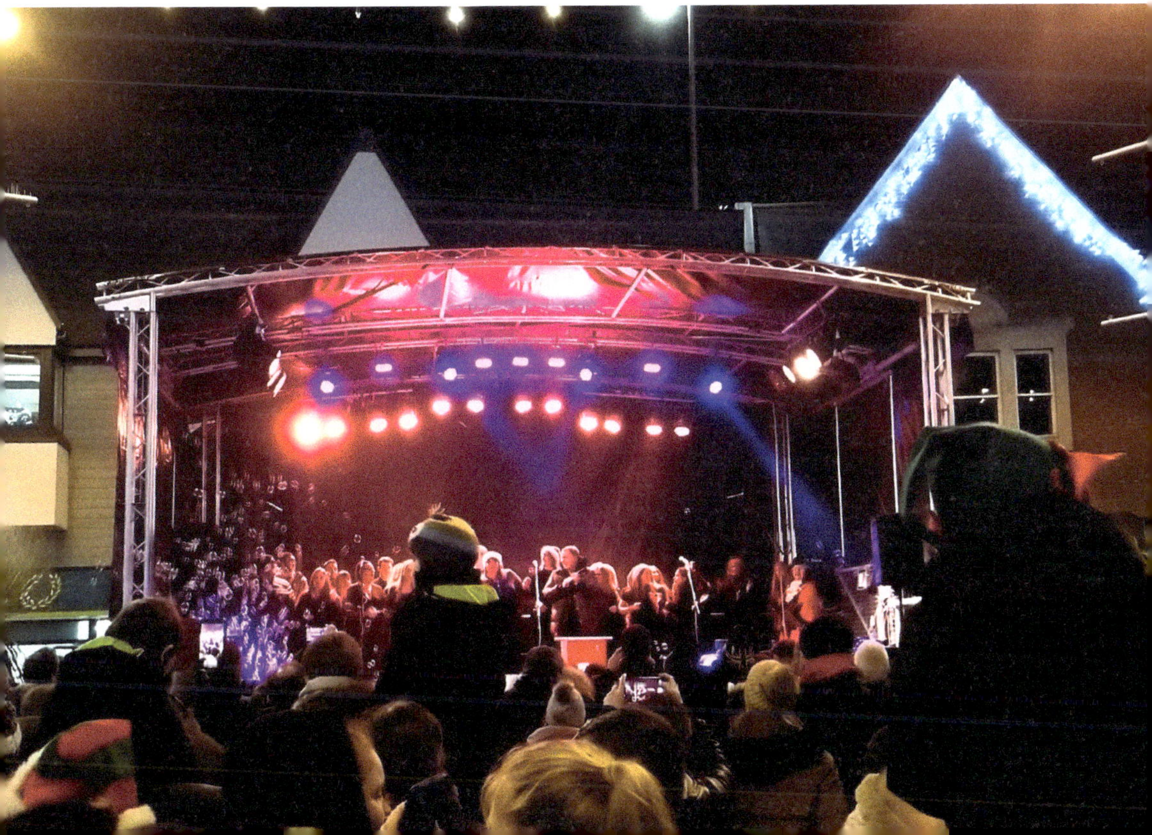

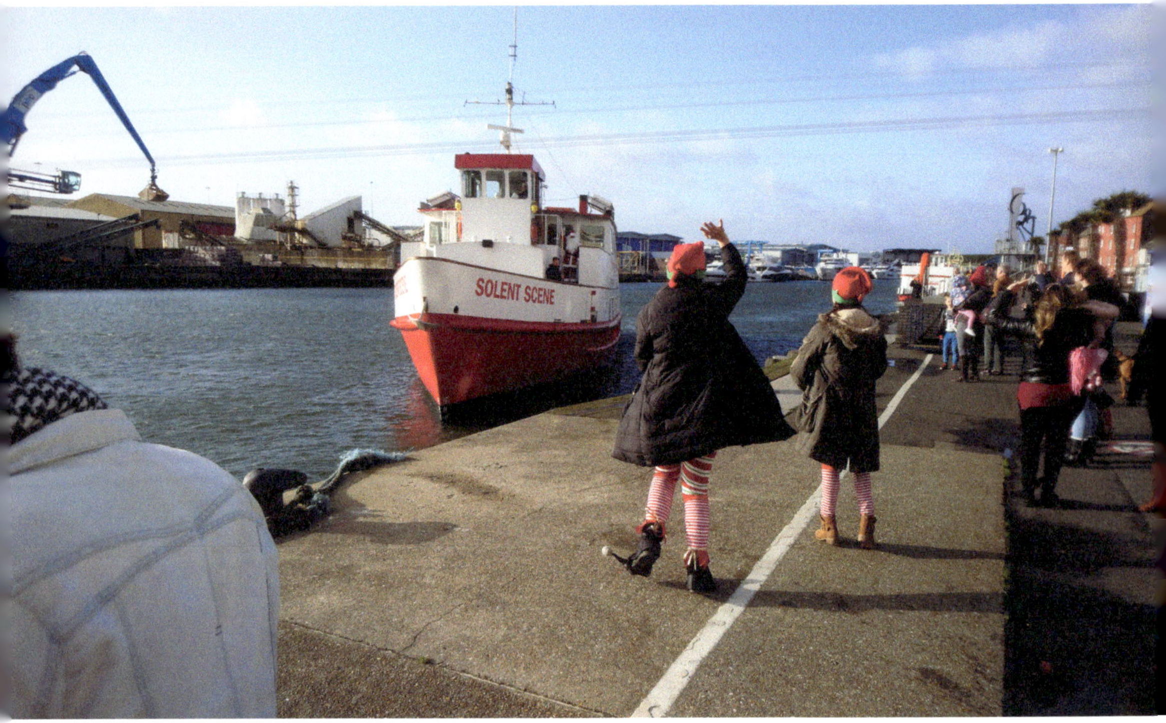

Above: The elves are excited to see Santa arrive by boat at the Quay.

Below: Another auspicious visitor takes to the stage.

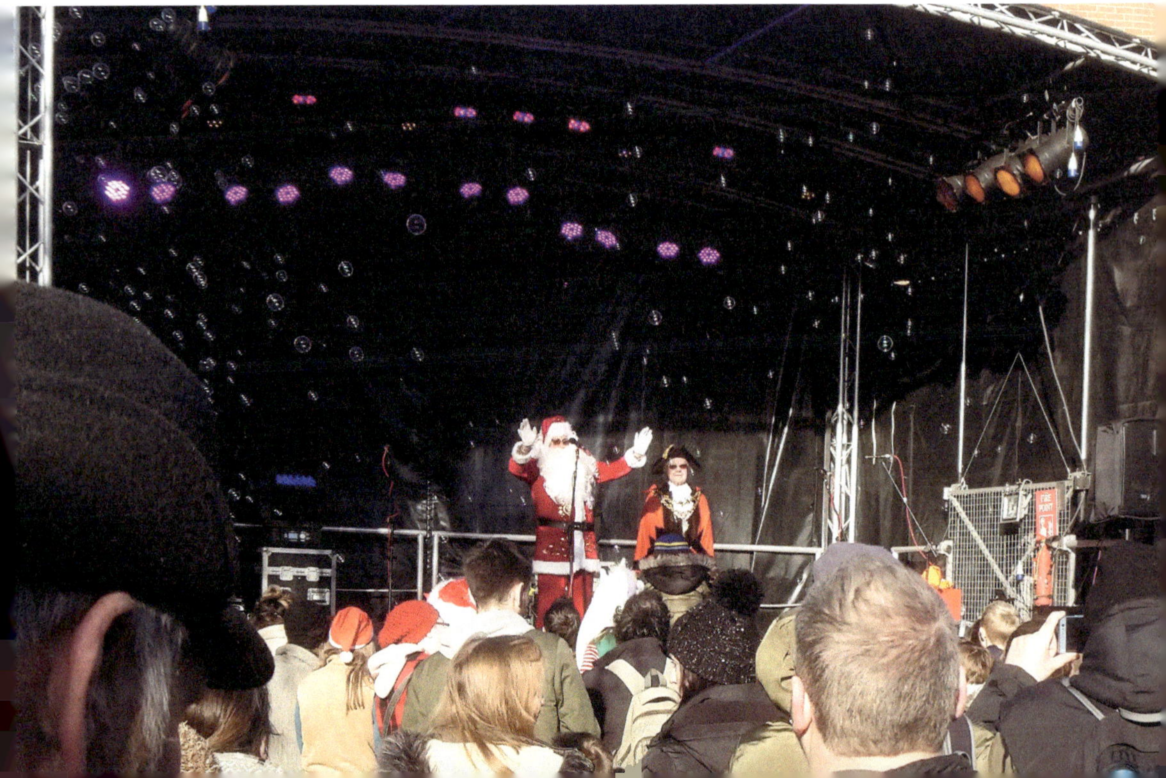

Y

Yacht Building

Ever since Iron Age man started building log boats, Poole has been a centre for boatbuilding. The tradition is nowhere more evident than at Sunseeker, who have been manufacturing high-performance motor yachts for the past fifty years and are one of Poole's greatest success stories. The company has won numerous awards including the Queen's Award for Enterprise.

The company which was originally called Poole Power Boats was founded in the 1960s by the Braithwaite brothers and was transformed when Henry Taylor, a boat dealer and Formula 1 driver, asked for a boat with a full-length sun deck. This prompted Robert Braithwaite to design the Daycap 23, which was a cross between a motor boat and a family cruiser. Since then, Sunseeker has developed into a global brand, as large and glamorous vessels roll off the production line for the world's rich and famous. They have even had starring roles in Bond movies.

Sunseekers roll off the production line.

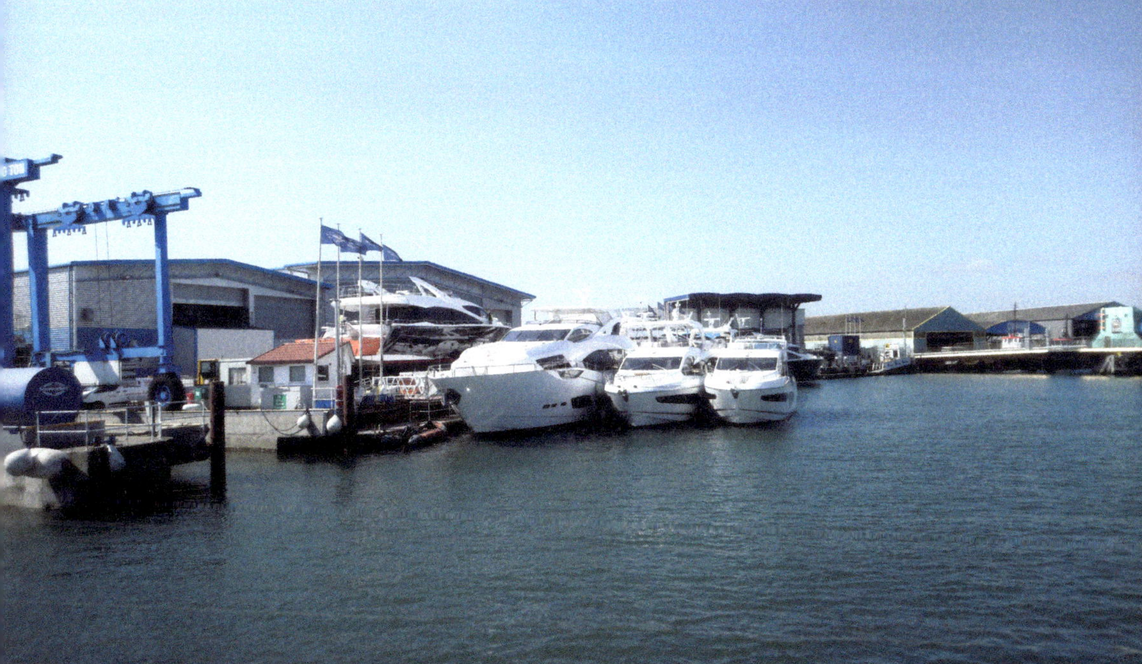

Another prominent boatbuilding yard was Bolson's, who prolifically built landing craft during the run-up to D-Day (see D-Day). They also built the cockleshell fold-up canoes used by the Cockleshell Heroes (see Cockleshell Heroes).

The business eventually closed in 1998, and became part of Sunseeker International in 1999.

Yacht Clubs

Poole is an ideal place for yachting enthusiasts to take to the water, and this is reflected in the fact that there are no fewer than seven sailing clubs:

East Dorset Sailing Club
Lilliput Sailing Club
North Haven Yacht Club
Parkstone Yacht Club
Poole Harbour Yacht Club
Poole Yacht Club
Royal Motor Yacht Club

In 2000, to celebrate the Millennium, the clubs combined to host and organise Poole Regatta. This was such a great success that it was decided to continue the event on a biannual basis.

Poole also hosts an annual boat show on the Quay, with a wide array of motor boats, yachts, RIBS, and stalls selling everything from water sports and boating equipment to clothing, training, tenders, trailers, engines and marine insurance. The main sponsor of the event is usually the 'Big Daddy' of the boating world – Sunseeker. The aim of the event is to get people on the water, and there are taster sessions available to enable people to do just that.

With so many sailing clubs in the town, it is no surprise that Poole regularly provides yachtsmen and women for the British Olympic team. However, to date Poole's most successful yachting Olympian is Rodney Pattison, who won gold medals for sailing at both the 1968 and 1972 Olympics in the Flying Dutchman Class.

Z

Zoo

In 1963, a zoo was established in Poole Park by brothers Frank and Ken Smith, in an area of the park which since before the First World War had been an aviary for exotic wildfowl. It was only a small zoo, but included such exciting creatures as wallabies, monkeys, a puma, a lion, a leopard, a chimpanzee, a black Himalayan bear and a giant tortoise on which children could ride. Also among the exhibits were some peacocks, whose loud cries were so annoying for neighbours that they were banished to Brownsea Island, where their relations still exist today.

What was especially thrilling for small children was to go on the miniature Poole Park railway, from which you could see some of the animals as you went round.

The zoo closed in 1994, as zoos at this time were generally out of favour.

Bibliography

Andrews, I., *Poole* (Phillimore, 1994)

Andrews, I. and F. Henson, *Images of England: Poole, The Second Section* (Tempus Publishing, 2000)

Burdett, D., *Poole: A Portrait in Colour* (The Dovecote Press Ltd, 2008)

Cullingford, C., *A History of Poole and Neighbourhood* (Phillimore, 1998)

Darvill, T. and B. Dyer, *The Book of Poole Harbour* (The Dovecote Press Ltd, 2010)

Guttridge, R., *Poole: A History and Celebration* (The Francis Frith Collection, 2004)

Hawkes, A., *A Pint of Good Poole Ale: Poole's Inns, Taverns and Breweries* (Poole Historical Trust, 2009)

Hawkes, A., *Book of Poole Quay and Waterfront* (Poole Historical Trust, 2013)

Hilliam, D., *The Little Book of Dorset* (The History Press, 2010)

Jackson, A., *Poole Pubs* (Amberley Publishing, 2019)

Jenner, L., *The Monmouth Rebellion and the Battle of Sedgemoor 1685* (Somerset County Council Heritage Service, 2007)

Levy, R., *Book of Poole Harbour and Town* (Halsgrove, 2005)

Richards, A., *Slow Travel Dorset* (Bradt, 2015)

Tincey, J., *Sedgemoor 1685: Marlborough's First Victory* (Pen and Sword, 2005)

50 Walks in Dorset (AA, 2009)

Leaflets
Art Detective, Poole Museum
Harbour Trail, Poole Flying Boats Collection
Poole Cockle Trail, Pooletourism.com
Poole trail. Pooletourism.com
Poole Town Programme v Chelsea XI, 20 July 2019
Thomas Kirk Wright

Websites
Birdsofpooleharbour.com
Bournemouthecho.com
Dorsetancestrywebeden.co.uk
Flickr.com
Localhistory.org
Piratesofpoole.co.uk
Poolemuseum.org.uk
Wordpress.com
Winnower.com
Zoochat.com